Distillation Is Beautiful

ERIN ELDRIDGE

DISTILLATION IS BEAUTIFUL
by
Erin Eldridge

Copyright © Erin Eldridge 2020
Cover Copyright © Kitty Honeycutt (Ravenswood Publishing)
Published by Veritas
(An Imprint of Ravenswood Publishing)

VERITAS

Ravenswood Publishing
1275 Baptist Chapel Rd.
Autryville, NC 28318
http://www.ravenswoodpublishing.com
Email: RavenswoodPublishing@gmail.com

Paperback orders can be placed through Amazon
http://www.amazon.com

Printed in the United States of America
First Edition
10 9 8 7 6 5 4 3 2 1

ISBN-13: 9798610446400

INSPIRATION FOR THE TITLE

Primo Levi is one of my favourite authors. An Italian Jew, he survived Auschwitz during World War 11 because he was a qualified chemist, and the SS put him to work in Buna, their rubber manufacturing plant in Monowitz camp, or Auschwitz 3. After liberation, he wrote some of the best Holocaust literature there is about his experiences. Primo loved the purity of science, and in one of his books, he used the phrase, 'distillation is beautiful', which resonated with me. I have applied it to the process of coming to terms with one's past.

INTRODUCTION

Somehow, the stork got the wrong instructions, or the wrong directions. Perhaps it was a mentally challenged stork, or it was near quitting time so it just off-loaded me down the nearest chimney. Anyway, if I could find that fucking stork I'd wring its scrawny neck.

Personal growth/self-awareness: at some point in your human journey, typically your more mature years, all the threads of your life braid together and cohere into a meaningful whole that splices your past and your present seamlessly to each other. This could be described as a watershed period, which involves much thoughtful reflection and where things begin to make sense at last, like stepping back from a neo-impressionist's pointillistic work of art and acknowledging that all of the little individual daubs of colour form a discernible portrait. It is an innervating process, during which all your life experience is distilled into clarity, and you can see unimpeded into its crystal clear depths, all the dross removed. Distillation is indeed beautiful.

Family: it's an emotive word, a loaded word. For many, it no doubt evokes warm feelings, fond memories, bittersweet nostalgia. For others, it is equivalent to hearing the words, "Fire!" "Wolf!" "Run for your life!"

Family is the biggest lottery, where you either win or lose, and makes nonsense of the frequently made claim that our own choices determine our life's outcome. You might have the good fortune to be delivered into a group of people with whom you have some affinity, or you may end up in the midst of a bunch of borderline psychopaths you wouldn't ordinarily give the time of day to. To paraphrase poet, John Clare: family are stranger than all the rest.

The culture in my family revolved around the three pillars of food, sport, and religion (Catholic, for us), as it did with most families in New Zealand in the golden years of the fifties. We skimmed over the surface of everything else, like tense skaters on dangerously thin ice. Emotion was forbidden. Sex was a taboo topic. (When my elder sister asked where she came from, she was told she'd been spotted perched on a cushion in A J White's department store, and subsequently purchased. I didn't bother to ask where I came from, mainly because I had no curiosity about the unpropitious circumstances that had seen me landed amongst this particular group of people. I also probably felt that if I'd been spotted on a cushion, I would have been bypassed. I was definitely an under-the-cabbages kid.) By the time my sister was nine months old, my mother was already pregnant with me. I don't think this helped me to gain a stable place in her affections. At the time, she was living with my father's relatives and dependent on their accommodation, in every sense. Managing two little ones and with a husband who was a star graduate of the prevailing hands-off-leave-it-to-the-missus school of paternity it can't have been easy. This was a period of rigidly defined, gender-based roles. Women gave up work when they married to cook, clean, keep house, and raise children, while men were the providers and undisputed heads of their families, greeted each evening with pipe, slippers and a home cooked meal. The Catholic Church, still a powerful force, stressed that wives must obey their husbands, especially in the bedroom, and bear lots of good little Catholics, sons being preferable as future candidates for the priesthood. Males were generally perceived as being superior to females in every sense. Gloria Steinem was still just a little girl.

Growing up in my family was a bit like being in boot camp. Any dissension, even protest against blatant injustice, was ruthlessly quashed. My mother's catchphrase, delivered with much hand wringing, was 'Keep the peace, for my sake.' To ignore such a *cri de coeur* would have been swinish. And so we lived, like little mayflies, skittering over life's surface while the currents swirled dangerously beneath us, sucking down the truth of who we really were, leaving us like empty cicada shells, while we desperately pretended everything was jolly and nice. *"The farmer's in the dell, the farmer's in the dell. Hey ho the merryo, the farmer's in the dell."* Pity his harvest was such a bitter one.

But enough retrospection. It's time to tell the whole story as it unfolded, the full tragi-comedic tale, with undertones of horror, that was my life growing up in my family. Hopefully, the remaining members will not be too discomfited by my version of events. If that is not the case, I welcome them to write their own memoirs to countermand mine. After all, each of us brings a unique filter to the process of distillation.

HOME FROM THE WAR

Apparently, my father joined up to fight Hitler before it was even fashionable. That is, before he was conscripted. He left my mother with no visible means of support, no roof over her head, and voluntarily hiked it over to England to join a New Zealand Air Force squadron, #75, based in Cambridgeshire, where, if his wartime diaries I later read were anything to go by, he had a high old time. Not in the air, you understand, a glamorous, moustachioed Battle of Britain pilot. No, he managed to secure a very safe job behind a desk and partied hard for nigh on six years. He was moustachioed, though.

Once the initial shock of abandonment passed, my mother, who had never worked at anything apart from waiting hand and foot on other people, most recently my father, was dismayed to find herself drafted into the WAAFs, (Women's Auxiliary Air Force) where she was put in uniform, handed a pinny, and told to get to work rustling up victuals for the cranky and perennially ungrateful trainee pilots at Wigram Air Force Base in Christchurch. Astonishingly, in those times of rudimentary contraception, my parents had already been married six years and produced no offspring, although I believe there was one miscarriage. Thus, my childless but able-bodied mother became part of the war effort, and the WAAFs' barracks became her home.

So, while I do not wish to mitigate my father's war experience, I believe it was a pretty good one. If his stories that were repeated *ad infinitum* at the dinner table when we were kids growing up were anything to go by, while my mother squirmed with embarrassment, he pretty much defeated Hitler single-handed. He told us he'd grown his ugly little moustache to cover the scar from a wound he'd sustained. (I found out from his brother, my Uncle Jack, that he suffered the 'wound' falling through a box hedge when he was drunk.) He had a most unattractive mouth with thin, saurian lips, that always reminded me of Adolf Hitler's, and the moustache did serve to camouflage it a little. Anyway, following this train of thought, I wanted to suggest that he write the Kiwi version of Spike Milligan's *Hitler, My Part in His Downfall*, but I learned from an early age to beware of his temper, especially when he'd been drinking, which was a lot.

I was a very sensitive child, hypersensitive even, and things that happened, that I witnessed, stuck inside me like pieces of irretrievable shrapnel, while they ricocheted off my more resilient siblings. Although not particularly observant of things around me, I possessed from an early age the (future) writer's dark fascination with people, the art of remembering in fine detail what they said and how they behaved, the struggle to understand what motivated them and the forces that shaped them. I still recall with horror the carving knife thrown at my mother, leaving a jagged weal on the wooden kitchen door; the food dripping like lava down a wall into the shattered remains of the crockery strewn on the floor (dinner was not to his liking); the beatings; the punch that just missed my sister's face and drilled a hole into the plaster wall in the hallway; the heavy, lead-filled cosh shattering the deck chair on Christmas Day, a split second after my sister and I got our heads out of the way. Perhaps I could have forgiven those outbursts of unrestrained fury if my father had suffered badly during the war, but the men who did, didn't talk about it, and shunned violence.

My mother did not intervene in these fiery episodes, not even to defend herself, but remained on the periphery of

5

them, barely reacting, determined presumably to make the best of things and 'keep the peace.' Which, of course, was no peace, merely capitulation. Only once did I ever see her stand up to my father, when he came at the younger of my two brothers with a coal shovel. She placed herself between them, screaming at him to stop. I think she knew that, with a weapon, he could produce horrific results. That was the only time I saw her display any gumption, and her intervention worked; my father backed off. I think he was as shocked by her uncharacteristic courage as I was.

So, my father was a hard-drinking tyrant and a bully, as small men often are. But, perhaps it was not always so.

PAT'S STORY

I was born in Balclutha, Otago province, in 1907, the youngest of seven children, and the fourth son. By the time I was born, my Irish mammy, Mary, didn't want to know, especially as she was forty-four years old and burning with resentment against my father. She left my upbringing to my three elder sisters, and I defended myself as best I could against my three elder brothers who made teasing me their favourite sport. My name was actually Howard, after an uncle who'd served in the Royal Irish Guards, but as I grew up I became Pat. Every Irish family has a Pat. The title usually designates the dull-witted one who was dropped on his head as a babby.

My father was a tall, dignified, good-looking man named John Anderson, with one serious flaw: he declined to work, and with seven kids to feed, this was a significant drawback. Eventually, sick of a diet of porridge and cabbages, and severely disillusioned with the marital condition, my mammy moved us off our farm, which was really a couple of acres of wretched, non-productive soil with a shack, and into Balclutha township where she opened a boarding house and sidelined my father to assistant status after banishing him from her bed so that no more babbies eventuated. By this time, she was recognised as the undisputed head of the family and afforded the respectful title 'The Mater' in acknowledgement of the fact. (My father's title, 'The Boss', was, I presume, ironic.) Squat, pugnacious, her body coarsened and broadened by continual childbearing, she bulldozed aside anything and everyone who got in her way with the single-minded determination of a rogue tank, but she held the family together.

The Mater's life had been a hard one. To escape her native Ireland and the horrors of the Great Starvation, compounded by British indifference to the suffering of the Irish people, she'd become one of the thousands who left to try their luck elsewhere in the colonies and had washed up in New Zealand on the Dunedin docks at the age of eighteen, full of optimism in a colonial boom time that promptly evaporated into economic depression. During a period when being a woman alone was not a good idea, she'd married a young journeyman of Swedish descent, my father, who apparently performed well in the sack – well, was definitely fertile, anyway – but unfortunately did little else that was constructive. Mum actually lobbied for and secured a labouring job for him at one point, and he set off after breakfast with his modest packed lunch, waving goodbye to Mary, who stood on the verandah with her brood tugging at her skirts, feeling that seductive old serpent, Hope, coil around the chambers of her heart. He was back by morning teatime, holding his hands out to her in the kitchen, his face contorted with indignation.

"Look at these. Filthy!" He retired to bed, the place where he was most active, for a rest.

I think Pop must have had a mid-life crisis at some point, because he announced that he was going to enlist for the Boer War. Whether this was inspired by a sudden uncharacteristic yearning for adventure, a desire to escape his growing responsibilities along with Mary's compounding bitterness, or a rather extreme attempt to earn some income we'll never know. While she may have been understandably tempted to get rid of him, Mam nonetheless put the kibosh on his dreams of military glory in no uncertain terms – perhaps there were still some vestiges of affection there – and he despondently resumed his role of sporadic provider. When World War One broke out, he was too old to enlist.

So, we were very poor. I remember the long walks to school in bare feet, winter and summer, the meagre food, the cast-me-down clothes. I remember the Christmas my elder brothers put a lump of coal in the stocking I'd attached to the mantle with aching optimism, and how they fell about laughing when the true identity of the alluring bulge was revealed to me under my trembling, groping fingers, morphing the expression on my face from joyful anticipation to one of devastation watered by hot tears of outrage. I made a mental note to always make Christmas a time of equal misery for any offspring I had in the future. (I, Erin, inserted that because he always ruined every Christmas we had with his vicious, drunken bitterness, his hurtful ingratitude for every gift he was given, and the story of the coal in the stocking was told *ad nauseam*. Thus, I have quite justifiably, I believe, made the link.)

After we finally abandoned the farm and moved into Balclutha, 'Big River Township' which was starting to boom, life improved somewhat. Mainly through swallowing her pride and making judicious use of charity handouts from our local parish, as well as doing other people's laundry, Mam had somehow saved £200, enough money to purchase an old but well preserved dwelling, which we converted as cheaply as possible to a boarding house. She'd worked in a boarding house in Dunedin following her arrival from Ireland and knew the basics of running such an establishment. Most of our boarders were young single men, which pleased my sisters, and were employed at the local Finegand freezing works.

This change of circumstances enabled our by now formidably hardened matriarch to take full charge of and oversee the family fortunes, while my father was reduced to a shadowy figure on the peripheries of this new milieu, quite redundant to all intents and purposes. The quality of our meals improved with our new capitalist status, and I began to grow a little, although I was still small. My sisters skivvied diligently, while my brothers exasperated Mam as they worked their way through the profits with their prodigious appetites for food and liquor, contributing little in the way of honest labour, and I was dispatched to boarding school to get me out of the way – well out of the way, as it turned out.

The first school I attended was St Bedes College, up in Christchurch. It was a Catholic school for boys run by the Marist Fathers, who had a reputation for good scholarship and firm discipline. I soon exasperated them with my wayward behaviour, and I was eventually expelled for peppering the gymnasium roof with pellets from an air rifle I'd somehow acquired. Mam refused to give up on me and I was handed on to the Marist Brothers at Sacred Heart Boys' College in Auckland – even further away – where I continued to consolidate my reputation as a rascal. There was one big German Brother, Brother Fidelis, whom I particularly hated because his methods of discipline bordered on the sadistic, and because he seemed to have a particular dislike for me.

Mum had sent me ten shillings, and because I was always hungry, as only young boys are, and the boarding school rations were adequate but never truly filling, I determined to spend some of it at the fish and chips shop not far from the school. I was squeezing my way back through the gap in the hedge we used for all our forays out of bounds, when a large hand descended on my collar and I was dragged out of the shrubbery like a squirming pup to confront a grinning Brother Fidelis. He hauled me over to a nearby tree stump, and after relieving me of my warm, mouth-wateringly fragrant parcel, he ensconced himself on the stump, tore open the paper and proceeded to eat my fish and chips with slow, savouring indulgence, while I was forced to sit at his feet and watch, salivating copiously. When he'd finished, he licked each finger with equally slow, lingering satisfaction before he marched me back to the dorm and caned me in his study. To complete my humiliation, he held me by the neck like a rabbit and snarled into my ear, "You mother doesn't pay your fees, brat. You are here on sufferance. Remember that."

Crying myself to sleep later, my heart burned with hatred and I began to plan my revenge.

Every morning after breakfast and before first lessons, all the boys congregated in the quad, waiting for the bell that announced the commencement of the school day. And every morning without fail it was Brother Fidelis who descended the stairs in a headlong flight, erupting out on to the verandah from the building's long passageway to snatch up the heavy brass bell that resided on a wooden table to the left of the broad concrete steps, ringing it vigorously and lengthily to underscore his control over us all. Watching him one morning, a fiendish smile on his broad, meaty face as he tolled away with his trademark flourish, the bell's clapper working furiously, an equally fiendish idea formed in my mind, and I found myself reciprocating the smile when our eyes briefly met. I knew in that moment exactly how I was going to get the bastard. First, I had to nick some materials from the woodwork room.

That night, I waited 'til all was quiet in the dorm before I slipped out of bed, glided wraith-like downstairs, along the passageway that led out to the verandah, unlocked the door and stepped out into the chill night air. I had a hand drill, some stout but pliable wire, and a hefty pair of pliers. Focused as a lion on its prey, I set to work. I enjoyed doing stuff with my hands and I liked a challenge, especially one that, if

11

successful, could wreak well-deserved revenge on an enemy. Task completed, I returned to bed, hiding the tools instrumental in my fiendish plot under my mattress before I snuggled down, feeling well pleased with myself.

The next morning, I made sure I was well positioned to witness Brother Fidelis's morning charge out on to the verandah to wield the bell that signalled another dreary day of lessons. He seemed to be in fine fettle on this particular morning as he erupted from the gloom of the hallway out into the sunshine, rubbing his hands with the joyful anticipation of disrupting our boyish socialising. As he drew abreast of the table, one large hand with its pelt of gleaming red hairs shot out to grasp the bell. I watched, breath held, as his vast paw closed around the handle and yanked viciously. The ensuing scream of agony transfixed every boy milling in the playground and a deathly hush descended as all eyes turned to the figure doubled over in obviously excruciating pain beside the bell table. I kept my face as expressionless as a death mask, while a few senior boys eventually detached themselves from the silent throng and sprinted to the brother's aid.

Serious ligament damage, that was the rumour. Weeks of wearing a sling and lots of Aspros for the pain. Some scallywag had attached a strong wire to the bell clapper and fed the other end through a neatly drilled hole in the table top before winding it tightly around a groove in one stout trumpet leg. Brother Gerard, the principal, summoned everyone to assembly and threatened us all with dire collective retribution if the culprit did not turn himself in. By this time, I had returned the tools to the woodwork room without a hitch, and after the initial period of outrage and feverish investigation the whole incident was quickly forgotten, confined to the annals of myth and legend associated with an all boys' school. In fact, there were many expressions of admiration for the inventiveness and boldness of the perpetrator, which I registered with smug satisfaction.

Whenever I passed Brother Fidelis in the quad, on the playing fields or in the corridors, I gave him the sweetest smile, and he, white sling contrasting starkly with his black soutane, would respond with a twitch of the lips and a narrowing of the eyes. He knew, and he knew I knew that he knew, but there wasn't a damn thing he could do about it. That was one of the sweetest triumphs of my adolescent years.

I was always immature, but most of my school years' pranks were pretty harmless, Brother Fidelis's trauma aside. Well, there was the ugly incident with the Jewish kid who cried inconsolably when I slipped ham into his sandwich, but I won't dwell on that. The lad that some accomplices and I trussed in a rope sling and dangled out the upper storey windows…well, that was a pretty harmless prank, really. At least we didn't drop him.

I didn't really distinguish myself in any way at school, other than as a reprobate, but I did achieve my Proficiency Certificate and then completed my subsequent two free years of secondary education. By this time, my family was in Balclutha, so I headed home to join them, without, I might add, much enthusiasm.

Life in Balclutha was predictably boring. I hooked up with some mates of a rather dodgy persuasion and went along for the ride when they converted a car. Being an underage felon, I ended up straddled across a table while being soundly birched by a large Otago policeman of a sadistic persuasion. This humiliation ended my criminal career and shortly afterwards the whole family headed up to the city of Christchurch to take over the proprietorship of the Star and Garter Hotel. Once again, The Mater did her best in the face of her lazy, hard-drinking offspring and ineffectual husband, but of course it all ended badly. Putting an Irish family in charge of large quantities of liquor can have only one outcome. We had to 'do a moonlight' to escape our creditors, hiding out for a while in dismal rooms above a Chinese restaurant and living from hand to mouth. Tui, my eldest sister, absconded to Australia with her Ocker paramour, Nell and Evelyn also married, and my two eldest brothers died from cirrhosis of the liver. *Quelle surprise*. The remainder of us ended up in an old manse on Durham Street, where once again we staved off poverty by taking in boarders. My remaining brother, Jack, crossed the ditch to Australia as well, where he married an Aussie girl. Nell, Evelyn, and I remained in Christchurch with our parents.

Meanwhile, Mam decided that I needed to find gainful employment. She dragged me down to the offices of the Press, Christchurch's leading newspaper, and I ended up with a steady job as an apprentice typesetter. With money in my pocket and keen to meet eligible young ladies, I set about fostering an active social life. One night, I ended up as something of an interloper at a private party on Flockton Street, where the booze flowed and the hostess, Gertrude, was famous for her crayfish salad. Gertrude also had a daughter who caught my eye. She was only fourteen, while I was nearly twenty, and her name was Dulcie. I started spending a lot of time with Dulcie, but I never called her that. To me, she was 'Bridgie'.

BRIDGIE'S STORY

I was born in 1913 to a young Tasmanian woman of convict descent who'd run away from home at sixteen, caught a boat to New Zealand, and fallen pregnant to a rootless young man who worked at the same hotel where she was employed as a waitress. My parents eventually married, but I did not learn I'd been born out of wedlock until years later when I applied for a passport. I was their only child.

When I was two years old, my father, who'd left home at an early age, like my mother, and had endured lots of hard knocks, joined up to go and fight in the First World War. He was in the Canterbury Mounted Rifles, the heavy cavalry, and fought in the Gallipoli campaign, where he was wounded, and later served on the Western Front until he was invalided home by troopship in 1917.

My mother and I were left alone and my mother took cooks' jobs at various places, including racing establishments. I loved to hang out around the stables and the horses and had a pretty happy childhood for the most part. That all changed when my father returned from the war, a shattered, dysfunctional man. Quite abruptly, I was sent to live with strangers, and although I was not treated cruelly, the pain caused by the rupture from my family, the sense of being worthless and unwanted, stayed with me all my life. I could rationalise it later by reassuring myself that my parents were going through a difficult time as my father readjusted to civilian life without the benefit of therapy, for what we would later call PTSD, after enduring the horrors of trench warfare for four years, but a child does not have that luxury. There were additional complications, too, I later learned. My mother actually did a stint in prison for procuring abortions.

Eventually, I rejoined my parents and faced the next big adjustment in my life: going to school. I was a mouse of a kid, lacking all confidence, and the bullies soon latched on to my vulnerability. Within the school boundaries, their persecution was subtle but persistent, but when they caught me alone at a bus stop one afternoon, they vented their cruelty without restraint. I was dragged up a driveway, stripped of my clothing, and beaten black and blue with sticks. When I arrived home traumatised and sobbing, my furious mother assured me, as she gently bathed my wounds, that she would accompany me to school the following day and settle with my tormenters. She was a big, raw-boned, formidable woman with a terrifying shock of unruly black, curly hair, and once she'd had things out with the headmistress, the bullying abruptly stopped, and I was left in peace.

I only had one teacher that I recall with any affection: Kate McIvor was her name. She suffered from arthritis, and all the while she was teaching she was squeezing a tennis ball she kept in her pocket to keep her hands from clawing up. One day, to my horror, she singled me out to answer a question she posed: What is a tunnel? I was so overcome with fright I blurted out, "It's a hole in a hill! It's a hole in a hill!" The class all hooted with laughter, but Kate quelled them sharply. "Dulcie is quite right," she asserted firmly. "That is exactly what a tunnel is." Yes, I liked her.

I got my Proficiency Certificate, but did not see any point in going on to secondary, as I hated school. I had a job, briefly, in Drayton Jones department store in the city, but I hated that, too, so in the end I just stayed home with my parents and kept house for them. They both drank heavily and were often incapacitated as a result. My father also suffered from high blood pressure, and since there was no treatment at the time he endured unbearable headaches, exacerbated no doubt by his alcoholic largesse. One time, he was so badly hungover that he inadvertently shut our curious new little ginger kitten in the coal range oven while retrieving the dinner Mum had kept for him, and suffocated it. I can still see him, crawling along the passage to his bedroom, crippled by the pain in his head.

We had a lovely Pomeranian dog that my mother adored called Paddy, and I took him on long walks with my best friend, Nancy. We loved to go to the kiosk tearooms in the Botanical Gardens, where Paddy would wait patiently, tethered outside, while Nancy and I enjoyed high tea. My life was pretty carefree, but I dreamed of a prince charming, as all girls do.

I met Howard when he came to a party at my home, and I fell for him right away, even though I was only fourteen and he was six years older than me. He started coming for Sunday dinner and as I grew older we went out more, to cabarets, the pictures, on picnics, and to the beach, and I got to meet his large family. We got engaged, and Howard bought me a gorgeous diamond ring with three dazzling stones from Stewart Dawsons. I was thrilled to my boots.

Howard had a motorbike so we had a lot of fun on that. He was there to comfort me when my father died at only fifty-two years of age. My mother lived over the brush with another man she moved in, but I don't want to talk about that. She died of a heart attack in 1945.

When I was twenty-one, Howard and I married, after I converted to Catholicism, and found our own little flat in an old two-storey house opposite the university in Worcester Street. Howard continued to work at the Press and I kept house, cleaned, and cooked for him. I loved to sit at the window with a cup of tea when my chores were done, watching the students come and go. Nancy had married, too, and often brought her little boy, Brian, to visit. Those were happy times. Then the war came.

PAT'S STORY

I wasn't going to wait for conscription to be drafted into some frontline infantry unit, so I voluntarily enlisted for ground crew in the Air Force as soon as war broke out and was shortly thereafter on my way to England to join the exclusively New Zealand squadron being formed there, the 75th. It was hard leaving Bridgie, but I knew my family would take care of her. She could move into the house on Durham Street with Mam, Pop, and Evelyn. As it turned out, she ended up in the WAAFs, and her letters were pretty positive about it all.

Once in England I was given the rank of Flight Sergeant because of my comparatively good education level and trained in supervision of armaments, specifically loading ordinance on to the bombers. I was like a pig in muck, honestly loved every moment of squadron routine and the English way of life: great pubs, quaint tearooms, picture theatres, musical shows, pretty WAAFs, like-minded mates, good food in the officers' mess, dances, welcoming locals inviting us into their homes. I had a grand time, punctuated by the odd episode of horror, for example a plane crashing on take-off or landing, returning all shot-up with crewmembers wounded or dead, or not returning at all. One incident that stayed with me was when we had to hose the remains of a tail gunner out of a Lancaster. Nothing left, just gore and guts.

My only surviving elder brother, Jack, was aircrew on another squadron and was shot down over Hamburg in the closing stages of the war. After he parachuted to safety, some German soldiers rescued him from a mob of civilians baying for his blood because they'd had a gutful of the saturation bombing by that stage of the war. They would probably have lynched him if they'd got their hands on him. Anyway, he survived a POW camp and at war's end returned to live in Australia, where he'd married Hazel and had one daughter, Merle.

My best mate on base was a good bloke called Dave Radley, who was also from Christchurch. He had an uncle who had promised to hand over his asphalting business to him after the war when he retired, and Dave asked me if I'd be keen to join him as an equal partner. I was quick to accept and we began to make plans for our post World War Two life, whenever that might be. We had big hopes for the business and were going to leave our mark on Christchurch for posterity in the form of quality paving ventures, lasting for the duration and forever associated with the prestigious name of Claridge and Tullet, the title of our firm, which already enjoyed considerable goodwill, according to Dave.

I arrived home on a troopship in December 1945, and Bridgie and I were reunited after six years apart. It was hard at first settling back into civvy life and having a wife to consider again. There was so much I missed about the war years, which had been pretty good to me. Bridgie and I moved back into Durham Street and I promised her we'd soon have our own place. Our first child, Cheryl, was born nine months after my return. The country still had rationing and things were tight, but Dave and I launched into our new road-building enterprise with high hopes for a bright future. We had big dreams, back then.

BRIDGIE'S STORY

When Howard left for the war, I was devastated. I didn't even have a roof over my head as I couldn't manage the rent for the flat on my own with no income, and I didn't want to live with his awful family at Durham Street, especially his horrible old mother. After a recommendation from a friend, I got a live-in position housekeeping for an elderly gentleman who was of sober habits, quiet, polite, and respectful. He was well off, owned a car, and was a prominent member of the Masonic Lodge. Sometimes, he travelled to the Lodge in Ashburton and when he did so he stayed there overnight. I liked it when that happened because I had the place to myself. He wasn't burdensome or anything like that. I just enjoyed the peace and quiet and being alone for a while.

I was happy and content there until the war caught me up in its dragnet, too. As I had no children (Howard didn't really want them. I had one miscarriage in the six years we'd been married.) I was drafted into the Women's Auxiliary Air Force, given my uniform, and posted to Wigram, where they were training pilots for the air war in Europe. I could have had an administrative position with my level of education, but I didn't want that so I was put to work in the pilots' mess and provided with living quarters on the base. I'd never really worked at a proper job, apart from the brief stint in Drayton Jones, so it was a bit of a shock to the system. However, I soon began to enjoy the camaraderie of the other women and made some good friends. Working in the mess suited me, since that's all I'd known, really: cooking, cleaning, serving. All my workmates were easy to get on with, and we had some great laughs.

On a Friday evening, we'd go into town and have a fish supper at Fails Café for a special treat. It felt good being independent and having my own proper money for the first time in my life. I opened a savings account at a bank in the city and began to put away regular amounts for our future life when the war was over. Howard sent some money home, too, and I saved all of it. I was determined to get our own home after the war and not be dependent on anyone else. Neither of us knew what it was to own a real home. My parents had always rented, and Pat's mostly had, too.

So, I settled into my part in the war effort and looked forward to letters from Howard, who from all accounts was having a high old time in England. He sent me a little brooch: a tiny fighter plane moulded out of an English sixpence. A friend of his in the squadron made them to give as gifts. It wasn't much, but I treasured it just the same. For my part, I sent him food parcels when the strict rationing allowed. He loved to get a fruitcake, which I made by substituting honey for sugar and a bit of lard for butter. What I loved was the company of the other women, being part of the 'gang', feeling accepted and being included in the conversation, though I mostly just enjoyed listening. I'm ashamed to say it, with the war and all the suffering that was going on, but for the first time in my life I had a sense of freedom, of belonging.

The years passed and finally the war ended. Howard sent word that he was on his way home. I was demobbed and moved into Durham Street with my in-laws. I found out that my sister-in-law had pretty much plundered all the items of clothing I'd left there in my glory box. She never admitted it, but one morning when I looked down at her feet I realised she was brazenly wearing the beautiful pair of silk slippers I'd bought before the war and tucked away for future use. I didn't make a fuss. What was the point?

Then Howard arrived home, and before I knew it I was pregnant. He was so sex-starved after six years that he didn't want to practise withdrawal anymore. He wasn't cut out to be a father, though. Not then, not ever.

PAT'S STORY

The journey home by troopship, via the United States, was the final chapter of my wartime adventure, and I enjoyed it for the most part. The big downside was that it was packed with returning servicemen and the demand on the hygiene facilities, like the showers, was heavy. Coming down through the tropics, we were hit with a hugely impressive rainstorm, the curtains of water so dense that visibility was severely curtailed. I had a brilliant idea, sprinted to my berth, grabbed soap and towel, and found myself a place on the deck to enjoy a wonderful shower courtesy of Mother Nature. I'd stripped off and was in mid-ablution when the rain abruptly stopped as if someone had turned off a tap! Catcalls and whistles soon followed as my nakedness was exposed to all. I hastily seized my towel and beat a retreat, crimson with embarrassment. I got teased about it for the rest of the voyage.

Settling back into civvy life wasn't easy, and I had a wife to consider again after leading a bachelor existence for six years. I returned to the Press for a while, to my old typesetting job. Rationing was still in place, and although my sister, Evelyn, did her best feeding us all, we were always hungry. When I finished my night shift, I'd buy two dressed pies from the pie cart in Cathedral Square, and Bridgie and I would devour them together in our room. She was pregnant, and a slice of bread and a bowl of soup for dinner just didn't cut it.

However, Dave and I gradually got involved in setting up the asphalting business he'd inherited, so that kept me busy.

I knew Bridgie wasn't happy living with my family, but there wasn't much I could do about that in the meantime. Our first child, a girl, was born in September 1945, and nine months later Bridgie was pregnant again. We both hoped for a boy. Looking after kids meant Bridgie had something to occupy her while I got on with the business of being the provider. There was a feeling of optimism in the air. Everyone was having families, there was work aplenty, and the economy began to boom, as war-strapped Britain couldn't get enough of our goods, especially agricultural products. Building new homes and suburbs started apace. Dave and I had inherited a good work team, two trucks, and sundry other bits and pieces of equipment. Everybody got along well, and we felt the sky was the limit: from driveways, footpaths, to roads and bridges, we were going to build it all!

In March 1947, we had a second daughter and called her Erin, as requested by my Irish mam. Bridgie didn't cope too well with two under two, and Cheryl went into care for a while until she got on her feet. When the baby was a year old, I won a house in a returned servicemen's ballot, and in autumn 1948 we moved into our first proper home.

MY STORY
Chapter One

I was born a little over eighteen months after my elder sister, Cheryl, and I believe this fact did me no favours within the family hierarchy, even though the event in question was entirely out of my control. My mother's limited psyche had been seriously affronted by this untimely conception, and I believe it made her subconsciously resent me for the rest of her life. The fact that I was not the anticipated son didn't help either, and my father emphasised his disappointment by nicknaming me 'Billy'. (In the womb, I was 'Jimmy', apparently.) However, for five years I remained the younger child and was therefore afforded the leeway, if not the affection, attached to this status. Not by my sister, though. She made it very clear that, as far as she was concerned, I was sibling dross and she was my overlord.

By the time I was old enough to start forming any memories, we had probably been at 219 Knowles Street in St Albans for two or three years. By the time I was aware of my surroundings, the area had become quite a built-up suburb, mostly peopled by ex-servicemen and their families, like my father. His ex-RAF buddy and business partner, Dave Radley, lived around the corner in Jameson Avenue, and Dave's brother-in-law, Gerard Fogarty, lived with his family just a few houses along from us. All three families eventually had four children, comprising two boys and two girls. Most post-war families tended to be quite large. A family who lived on the corner had eight wild boys, their mum ending up in a mental institution, while a school friend was one of seven daughters. A boy called Bevan who lived in the next street was regarded as an oddity, being an only child. Everybody lived in the same style of wooden bungalow, with variations, on a quarter acre section, frequently with a chicken coop. Some who were better off built brick homes, or, more rarely, two storey houses, which we considered a sure sign of wealth and prestige. Most houses did not have a garage, since so few owned cars at the time.

Mum said when they first moved to our house, it was surrounded by paddocks, and the cat was always bringing in lizards and other wildlife. However, by the time I was old enough to explore my environs, there were lots of neighbours and everyone had their picket fences up, paths laid, vegetable gardens in, and lawns sowed. The nearest shops were about a kilometre away at Westminster Street, and Mum would push me and my sister up there in the pram, one lying prone, the other perched on a board that straddled our conveyance, to a kind of general store owned by a kindly man called Mr Woodham. Eventually, we got our own cluster of shops just around the corner, and Mum was beside herself with excitement. There was a butcher, a grocer, a cake shop, a drapery, a gift shop, a dairy, a fish and chip shop, a chemist, and a bookshop, my favourite. When we were older, my sister and I loved to read the kids' comics and spent most of our pocket money on them; most coveted were 'Schoolfriend', 'Girls' Crystal', 'Chicks' Own' and 'Sunny Stories'. Occasionally, we chose 'Beano' or 'Dandy'; Desperate Dan and his cow pies amused me no end. The Disney comics, especially Donald Duck and Uncle Scrooge, were favourites, and, once we were older, 'Superman' and 'Batman'. The latter were great for learning onomatopoeic words, like 'thwack', 'blam', and 'kaboom'.

I enjoyed the Classic Comics as well and built up quite a vast collection, which I stored in a box under my bed. They were beautifully drawn and provided my pictorial introduction to many classic works of literature like *Kidnapped, Lorna Doone,* and *Macbeth.* What also made them special was their unique sour papery smell that added to their allure and never failed to stimulate my senses. Books have always given me a visceral thrill. I get a real rush when I enter a library. Most of the kids swapped their comics around, but I guarded all mine jealously, reading and re-reading them, while keeping them in pristine condition. Eventually, Dad threw them all out. Fathers are unsentimental in that way. Our toys were ruthlessly culled as well.

Our second favourite shop was the dairy, where we bought such exotic fare as all day suckers, licorice pipes and sherbert. All day suckers didn't quite last all day, but we loved to perch on the coal box on a sunny afternoon licking away in blissful silence until they turned to fragilely transparent red slivers, barely clinging to their sticks. Our tongues would turn red also.

Mum favoured the cake shop, run by a tiny frazzled little woman with dark curly hair, and we were often despatched to purchase kiss cakes, battenberg, and afghans. She also patronised Mr Common's Four Square grocery shop, putting in an order every week. Over the summer, we were often despatched to this shop to purchase 'half a pound of ham and half a pound of 'roundy' meat' (Belgian or luncheon sausage) for an easy summery meal. I frequently got the job of peeling away the filaments of red plastic seal from the rim of each circle of pale, processed sausage, before it was served. Mum would boil potatoes and make a salad to go with this exotic fare, serving it with mayonnaise formed by adding vinegar and mustard powder to a tin of sweetened condensed milk. Sounds odd, but it actually tasted really good. Most of our vegetables came from the garden since we had no local greengrocer, but once a week an itinerant supplier, Mr White, called by in his van, and Mum bought fruit from him. I loved greengages and passionfruit.

I think Dad's favourite shop was the butcher's. Mum said he was so 'meat hungry' when she first met him, because of the poverty he'd mostly grown up in, and he was certainly very specific about what cut of meat was to be bought for his dinner on any particular night. Once a week Mum made him a lamb curry while we kids had something else, and he loved offal, too, like sweetbreads and liver, oddly nostalgic hangovers from his deprived childhood, I guess. He was also passionate about tripe and onions, the sight and smell of which we found disgusting. Mum would mutter rebelliously when he demanded these dishes that his Irish mam had traditionally made for him, and which also frequently included Irish stew, potato scones, dumplings, and big pots of beef bone soup. She always had to add a dollop of mashed potato to his soup bowl, or she'd hear about it. She'd never liked his mother very much, so I guess that didn't help. Gran, according to Mum, overcooked everything and – cardinal sin – actually put baking soda in her peas, which, while it may have made them brilliantly green, also made them slimy. There was quite noticeable culinary competition among housewives in those days, and recipes were jealously guarded or swapped with family and friends. Women were frequently assessed as 'wonderful cooks', 'beautiful bakers', or, shamefully, 'lacking in the kitchen'. Mum self-effacingly described herself as a 'plain cook', but she was definitely above that.

On a Thursday, Mum would give the butcher a weekend meat order, and then one of us kids would traipse around to pick it up after school on Friday, staggering home with a huge brown paper wrapped parcel that included the Sunday roast. Sometimes, we had so much of that Sunday roast left over, that Mum would make shepherd's pie for Monday night's dinner. I loved to help her clamp the old fashioned meat grinder on to the table edge and turn the handle to feed through the big chunks of cold roast meat along with onions and any left over veges, mixing through any unused gravy, and topping the whole savoury mass with mashed potatoes, which she scored with a fork to make sure they browned nicely. One of my favourite treats as a kid was lining up with my siblings to receive a share of the rich, dark jelly that formed under the fat Mum drained from the roasting pan. It was delicious.

Like all families in the fifties, we ate a lot of meat, but whenever I went to friends' places for tea, or stayed with relatives, I realised that we ate a lot more than most. We had one cousin who was vegetarian, and he was regarded as a freak of nature.

As if the excitement of getting our own local shops wasn't exciting enough, the tram service was extended to our neighbourhood, too, and this was how we commuted to the city, a place of dazzling allure and excitement, a trip to which always engendered great excitement and anticipation. Late night was Friday, before everything closed down for the weekend, and we loved to see the lights of the city and be part of the bustle of shoppers between 6 and 9 p.m. Our favourite stores to visit were Ballantynes, DIC, Hays, and Beaths, and, of course, Mackenzies and Woolworths for cheap, gaudy bric-a-brac. Ballantynes had been rebuilt after a devastating fire the year I was born, and which had resulted in the deaths of forty-one people, most of them women.

Our house was small, only two bedrooms, so Cheryl and I had to share, sleeping together in a double bed. There was a little sunroom at the front entrance, a dining room, a washhouse (laundry), a bathroom, and a separate toilet, which was situated miles away from the bedrooms at the end of the washhouse, making it a real mission if you got caught short during the night.

Houses didn't yet include a shower, just a rather large bath tub, and everybody, including us kids, only bathed every few days or so. 'Bath night' was a special occasion and included a vigorous shampoo. In between bath nights, we used a large shared flannel for a 'proper wash' over the hand basin.

The dining room was called 'the breakfast room' for some obscure reason. We ate all our meals there, not just breakfast. We had a lounge but did not use it, as it was bare and uncarpeted, our parents having run out of funds for furnishings. We lived in the breakfast room for the most part, huddled over the small open fire in winter. It was a very badly laid out house, but typical of the post-war bungalows springing up. Mum used to say it was "jerry built".

My mother cooked on a narrow green and white enamelled Atlas stove that stood on four spindly little legs and had thick, solid, black elements on top. They took forever to heat up, but were brilliant for pikelets. Mum would smear butter all over the biggest hotplate and cook the pancakes right on it. Our aged cat loved to sleep in the little alcove under the stove because it was nice and warm there, when the oven was on.

I remember we had lots of power cuts post-war, and Mum had to cook over the fire with our only light provided by an old kerosene lamp. I adored this camp style adventurism, but it must have been hard on Mum. Men and women had clearly defined roles and men were providers who didn't help with any aspect of 'women's work'. We didn't have a refrigerator; no one did. We had a meat safe, a kind of sloping box built into the kitchen wall and projecting a couple of feet beyond the outside wall of the house. It was roofed with tiny wooden shingles and had fine mesh grilles inserted in the side panels to allow air to circulate while keeping insects out. On special occasions, like Christmas and Easter, Dad would arrange to have blocks of ice delivered to preserve the extra quantities of food the celebrations demanded. These blocks sat in the two concrete tubs in the washhouse, with hams, chickens, geese etc wedged around or on top of them

Laundry day was literally that. It took a whole day to do the family clothes wash, such was the labour involved, and Mum started early, straight after breakfast. First, she chopped wood into kindling and, along with screwed up newspaper, used it to light a fire under the copper cemented into a corner of the washhouse. As the fire got going, she ladled pails of water into the copper and added soap, shaving slivers off a big yellow bar of Sunlight with a vegetable knife. When the water was boiling, Mum added the clothes, and whatever else she needed to launder, into the copper and stirred it all vigorously with a big wooden paddle, in between feeding more wood into the fire to keep it stoked. Then the washed garments had to be ladled into the nearest of the two big concrete tubs beside the copper, and swirled around in cold water before being put through a heavy mangle that dropped them into the second tub, ready to hang. When all this was done, Mum, by now red-faced and perspiring, took the clothes outside in a big woven wicker basket to peg on the rope line, which was then hoisted into the air using stout wooden poles with grooves in the top to support the line, while their bottom ends dug on an angle into the turf of the lawn. The pegs were made of wood, and we used to make dolls out of them, drawing faces on them and dressing them in scraps of material.

Hand washing was done over one of the tubs, working the clothes vigorously up and down against a semi-submerged wooden washboard with galvanised metal ribbing. Mum used bluebag to whiten the whites, and if a kid got a bee sting, which happened frequently as we played outside so much, the bluebag doubled as a treatment for that. Held against the stung area, it soothed the pain.

Eventually, to her joy, Mum got an agitator washing machine and a rotating clothesline. There was fierce competition to have these latest work saving gadgets, and we kids boasted amongst our peers when our families acquired new appliances, coveted status symbols. My family's excitement was immense when we finally got a large bulky, fridge, and the old meat safe was surgically removed. As well, the double bed my sister and I slept in was replaced by two singles, in recognition of our growing need to each have our own space, even if we still had to share a room. Very few of our friends had their own room.

Every home had a good-sized vegetable garden to keep the family supplied with peas, potatoes, beans, tomatoes, cabbages, carrots, silverbeet, lettuce, and onions. I was a proficient thief of the peas, hunkering down between the rows to conceal my pillaging and gorging on the sweet, plump pods. This was generally indulged until my exasperated father hauled me out and sent me packing before his crop was decimated.

There were flower gardens aplenty, too, and neighbours vied with each other to produce the best displays. My mother loved flowers, and it would have provided a nice interest for her to be able to propagate her favourites, like pansies, daisies, roses, and lilies. But this was forbidden by our father, who brooked no interference with his horticultural domain. He oversaw it with the same rigid discipline he applied to his family, and anything that dared send out a wayward shoot or raise its head above the proscribed border was ruthlessly dealt with. He did sow some of Mum's favourites, though, by way of concession. She especially loved the bleeding heart planted under their bedroom window.

Saturday was the day traditionally devoted to gardening in our neighbourhood. Unless it rained, everyone would be out mowing, weeding, sowing, pruning, hoeing, and clipping, according to seasonal demands. Afterwards, mums got the tea on, while their men went off to the pub for the evening binge, and to 'fill the jar' for Sunday. Life was predictable and secure, bound by familiar rituals.

There were lots of other kids in the neighbourhood as the post-war baby boom gathered momentum, and we were never short of friends to play with, although you had to watch out for the neighbourhood bullies, in our area two unpleasant brothers, Brian and David Hay, and a lad with an uneven crew cut whom we taunted as 'the broom man', running off with screams of terror when he came after us. The Hays boys got a nasty dose of ringworm and had to have all their hair shaved off. Their delighted victims enjoyed taunting them about their scabby heads – from a safe distance, of course. We roamed freely, knew everybody, and visited each other's homes, where the parents made everyone welcome with food, drink and playthings to share. Nuclear families were the norm, with a patriarchal structure taken for granted. Not a single one of our friends had a solo parent or a mother who worked. As each day drew to a close, wherever we were, we all scattered off home for our teas. Such was the communal spirit that all the adults went out to a restaurant one evening for a 'street dinner', and on occasions like Guy Fawkes night everyone got together to share their fireworks.

We had an empty section next to us for a while, and when a house was finally built on it we had loads of fun playing amongst the semi-completed structure on weekends or once the builders had finished for the day. All the neighbourhood kids gathered there to clamber about, and when Bubby Pearce pooed her pants playing on the foundations, we marched her back to her home across the road, one kid carrying the soiled knickers, bulging with their steaming load, ahead of us on the end of a stick. Bubby was whisked away for a hose down, and Mrs Pearce was very grateful we'd retrieved the knickers, as she had a large brood to keep in underwear, however abused. Eventually, the doors were put in on the house and we were locked out. A sweet elderly couple subsequently moved in, and we kept mum about Bubby Pearce shitting on their property.

The Pearces were one of the first families to move on, and their house was purchased by a pleasant, childless couple, the Lockhearts, who doted on my brother Michael. Of course. They owned a milk bar, and one Sunday they took us all into the city, which was in weekend lockdown, and opened up their business to treat us kids to an ice cream soda each. Soon, they moved on as well, buying a house on Cashmere Hills, which was considered a posh area. Most of the houses in our street changed hands several times, property being within everyone's grasp at that time, and making for fluidity of movement, but our parents clung doggedly on, residing at the same address until they died. When the boys were born, they added a third bedroom and, later, a garage.

We all had sandpits to get creative in with buckets and spades, and hooned about on our tricycles, scooters, and in pedal cars. A chain bike was considered the acme of sophistication, but they were expensive and only a privileged few owned one. We girls played dress-up and raided our mums' cosmetics to paint our faces. Boys dressed up, too, as cowboys or Indians, and chased us firing their cap guns or suction-tipped arrows. It was an era of very rigidly defined gender! A nearby creek was a favourite haunt or we went to the park and flew kites. Only the coldest or wettest of days kept us inside, where board games like Ludo, Snakes and Ladders, and Checkers kept us amused, and over summer we turned brown as berries, gleefully cavorting about on hot days under the water arcing out of the lawn sprinkler.

Raiding the neighbours' fruit trees they'd been unwise enough to plant in their front gardens saw us excel at hit and run. Mrs Reed's crab apple tree was a favourite one to hit. Sometimes, but not often, we were plain bored, which was also good life training.

Two boys lived directly opposite, the same ages as my sister and me. They became our 'boyfriends', Robert attaching himself to me, while his elder brother, Malcolm, was Cheryl's beau. We spent hours just roaming the neighbourhood together, and Robert always held my hand in his own sweaty small one. Malcolm as the eldest, and apparently the most sexually aware, orchestrated us in you-show-me-yours-and-I'll-show-you-mine, and we examined each other's genitalia with childish wonderment.

I was bereft when the boys' family eventually moved away. Robert was my first love, and we had made a pledge to marry in the future. Years later, when I saw him at university, he did not recognise me, and I was too shy to approach him.

Other pastimes we enjoyed were dressing up our aged cat, an elderly mouser called Harvey that our parents had acquired to keep rodent and reptile life under control when our neighbourhood was still semi-rural. We'd bundle him into babies' or dolls' clothes and tuck him into the pram, lying on his back, front paws neatly arranged side by side on the coverlet. He was the most good-natured cat ever and purred away while we pushed him around the neighbourhood wearing a baby's bonnet, telling startled old ladies who peered under the hood that he was our baby brother. Later, we dressed our real baby brother, Michael, up as a girl and touted him around the neighbourhood as our baby sister! Not sure what Mum was doing as we carried out these dubious activities.

Mum had a shocking-pink cantilevered sewing box and a big tin of buttons that we loved to play with, while her precious foot high statue of the Virgin Mary got the pram treatment also. A short green duster broom was transformed into a doll of sorts with long, stringy hair, and my sister and I played endless games involving a battle between good and evil forces represented by two imaginary friends called Good Clilly and Bad Clilly. Cheryl had another imaginary friend called the Poody Owl. She'd take a cushion down to our low front gate, arrange it like a saddle over the pickets, ensconce herself on it, and swing idly back and forth on the hinges, communing with Poody Owl, while sucking her thumb. This sent our mother into a frenzy, mainly because the neighbours could easily witness it. Mum was big on giving the neighbours no room for gossip or causing them any annoyance. It was all about keeping up appearances.

With our parents, we enjoyed many outings and adventures. Nobody had cars, except the wealthy, so Dad would bring one of the two work trucks home for the weekend, and while Mum sat up front in the cab, my sister and I snuggled up in rugs and on pillows in the back, with a complete disregard for child safety, which was not a concern in those days. Dad, who had trophies for clay pigeon shooting, was pretty skilled with a shotgun, and we went out rabbit shooting often. Mum always packed a picnic lunch and Dad was in charge of the thermette for boiling water and making tea in a billy. We kids got the job of foraging sticks to get the thermette burning. Any rabbits bagged went in the truck tray with us kids for the journey home and subsequently into a tasty stew. A good haul meant one or two were gifted to neighbours.

Sometimes we dressed up in our best finery and went to town on the tram. Going to a movie matinee at the beautiful, exotically furnished Regent Theatre in the Square was always exciting, and I habitually made a beeline for the large gilded cage at the foot of the lounge staircase which was home to the theatre's sulphur-crested cockatoo, a bird of wide renown, who greeted all patrons with a cheery 'Hello!'

At Christmas, we visited Pixieland on Hay's Roof and sat on Santa's knee to make our present requests. Mum frequently took us to DIC's for high tea in the elegant tearooms. The waitresses with their frilled aprons and starched caps delivered silver service to the tables, the crowning moment being the arrival of the tiered cake stand with its superb array of sandwiches, cakes and pastries. Following that treat, we'd visit Wardell's delicatessen to stock up on sausages, bacon, and pickles. I can still smell the interior of that shop: spicy, meaty, musky, exotic, with an undertone of scrubbed floorboards.

Christchurch's image as a quiet, peaceful, religiously conservative place was somewhat shattered when the news broke of the shocking Victoria Park murder in 1954. Two teenaged girls bashed the mother of one of them to death in the park, using a brick concealed in a stocking. I remember my parents talking about this dire event in hushed tones, but I didn't fully understand it until I saw Peter Jackson's movie, *Heavenly Creatures*, years later. The murder was, without doubt, a cruel manifestation of the dark underbelly lurking in New Zealand culture. A litany of equally hideous murders dogs our history. Then there are our appalling records for child abuse, domestic violence, male on female violence, drunk driving, youth suicide, school and workplace bullying, animal cruelty.

'God's own country'? I don't think so.

****

As a child I was constantly sick, which curtailed my activities somewhat. I had endless colds and bouts of tonsillitis, which confined me to bed and necessitated frequent visits from the family doctor with administrations of a noxious white liquid antibiotic, which tasted like the 'milk' you squeeze out of a dandelion. (At some point all kids just *have* to taste that milky substance that bleeds out of a broken dandelion stalk.) In addition to the dandelion milk, and having my snotty rags doused with eucalyptus oil, I was made to sit at the dining room table for long periods with my towel-draped head over a steaming bowl of pungent Friars' Balsam decongestant, while my father badgered me to 'breathe deeply'. Antibiotics aside, a much-lauded by-product of the war years, paediatric medicine was still pretty basic. Mum administered large doses of castor oil and a repulsive concoction called Milk of Magnesia. If you were constipated, you got Andrews Liver Salts, which, dissolved in water, was vile fizzy stuff that worked rapidly and had dire consequences for your fledgling bowels. If you had a cold, you were basted with Vicks Vaporub until your pyjamas became plastered to you like a layer of mummy wrapping. This is not to mitigate the fact, however, that medically speaking, we were indeed the lucky generation. Immunisation and antibiotics put an end to lethal childhood illnesses like diphtheria, whooping cough, and pneumonia, and we were also spared the horrors of tuberculosis and polio as vaccines developed. By and large, we were healthy, sturdy, robust kids. Not me, though, at least not in my early years.

Tissues hadn't been invented yet, so Mum cut up old sheets into large squares in an attempt to manage the copious amounts of mucous I generated. I had no appetite and was grievously underweight. My parents quarantined me to a single bed placed in a corner of the still-unfurnished lounge and close to their bedroom. Dad would light a fire in the hearth there, and I would lie in bed in the darkened room watching the glowing coals and flickering flames that kept the shadows at bay, my small body suffused by a feeling of warm lassitude. Talk of an operation was bandied about as I continued to struggle. To add to my misery, I developed a painful eczema behind my knees, which refused to clear up.

Chapter Two

The root of my difficulties with my family stemmed from the fact that I was an acutely sensitive, emotional child with a fertile imagination, and these particular qualities had no value for the people amongst whom I was assigned to live, indeed, seemed to aggravate them. My parents were Depression era down-to-earth pragmatists, and my sister was cut from the same cloth. I was painfully shy, but always eager for acknowledgement and empathy that, alas, did not eventuate. Physical needs, by and large, were tended to. Emotional ones were not. I don't recall a single loving touch, a single loving or kind word, any show of affection whatsoever. The tenderhearted, compassionate child, the romantic dreamer with so much love to give was the least valued, the most spurned. That was the essence of my tragic family placement.

I dreaded going to bed every night because I was terrified of the dark, even though I shared the room with my sister. As soon as I closed my eyes, the nightmares would begin, always the same, down to minute detail, strange, disturbing visitations that left me sweat-drenched, paralysed with dread.

I am on some kind of a litter or stretcher, being borne along by shadowy figures that I know bear me no goodwill. We halt in front of a brutal man who stands before a fire, which seems to be blazing in a large circular drum. He looks down at me and smiles, the smile

41

of a rapacious tiger. As his huge arms reach for me, I force myself awake, and lie rigid, heart pounding, eyes wide open to avoid further sleep.

When sleep does inevitably come again for a tired, growing child, I find myself falling from a vertiginous height into deep, sinister green water that I know will never release me once I plunge into its shadowy depths. To avoid the agony of drowning, I force myself to wake again, and once more lie prone and terrified until I am aroused from a final, unconscious doze.

I decided that the only way to keep these horrors at bay was to snatch my father's torch from his cupboard where he kept his personal bits and pieces and smuggle it into my bed. This ruse was, of course, quickly discovered when a parent checking on us before retiring for the night spotted an unearthly glow emanating from within my bed sheets, and I was punished accordingly. The terrifying phantasms continued to plague me every night until, when I reached a certain age, they came no more. In adult life, the nightmare that replaced them for a long time saw me running with desperation from a wall of approaching water, clinging to a post or tree while the surges buffeted me and swirled around me. Under my feet there is a tiled floor of an antique character; Greek or Roman? Did I perish in some ancient tsunami?

I have no doubt now that these recurrent dreams were visions of past lives. Or should I say, past deaths? I am a firm believer in reincarnation and know without a shadow of a doubt that I am a very old soul.

When I had children of my own, I ensured that they always had the soft, glowing comfort of a nightlight, and I do the same for my grandchildren when they visit.

My sister turned five and commenced her schooling, catching the tram of a morning with a few other local kids to travel to

St Mary's College on Colombo Street, a Catholic school built close to the city in 1894 and run by the Sisters of Mercy, who in those days wore the full, formal nun's habit including veil, white bandeau, white guimpe and full length black dress, giving them a formidable appearance for an impressionable child and commanding instant respect, if not outright terror.

I now had my mother's undivided attention for most of the day. At breakfast time, I collected the discarded bacon rind off my father's plate after he'd left for work, had a good gnaw on it, and then secreted the rubbery little strands under my pillow for additional snacking upon. Following this ritual, my mother gave me the scrambled egg pot and I scraped and scraped away with a spoon, until the pot was so clean that washing it was a mere formality. If the weather were warm, I liked to perform this exercise while seated on the back doorstep. For lunch, I had hot Bovril with cooked macaroni in it, my favourite. Dinner was always a mission as Mum had a mania for heaping everyone's plate with mashed potatoes, and I hated them, especially when she drowned them in a white, gluggy parsley sauce. One was expected to clean one's plate, which caused me untold agony. Meanwhile, my health battles continued.

Soon it was my turn to go to school. I was kitted out in a little blue linen frock that belted at the waist, navy blue cardigan, black blazer with momogram, brown knee-high socks secured with garters, brown sandals – the kind with bits cut out and closed toes – a white panama hat with blue band around the brim, silver badge in front, and an elastic chinstrap to keep it in place. I thought I was the bee's knees. A little brown suitcase completed my attire and housed my lunch and drink bottle. Beneath my uniform, I wore an enormous pair of baggy blue bloomers, a cotton singlet, and over the singlet a strange little garment called a bodice: a kind of sleeveless vest with a row of rubber buttons down the front. Its purpose still defeats me, as it was neither warm nor comfortable...just there. I eventually gave up bodices and graduated to locknit petticoats, soft clingy garments, which I usually tucked into my bloomers, defeating the purpose somewhat. These, too, were finally abandoned.

Since my fifth birthday fell in early autumn, all the kids were still in summer uniform, which was the variant I started off in. For the winter term, we wore a black pleated gymfrock, long-sleeved blue blouse and tie, jersey, and black felt hat with the same hatband and badge. Blazers and hats were always worn to and from school, and before entering class we hung them on a personally named peg in the cloakroom, leaving our bags or satchels on a bench beneath. Each child had a pair of slippers that remained in school and were lodged in named 'boot boxes'. These were compulsory wear in the classroom. For 'drill' (physical education) we had sandshoes, white canvas lace ups with rubber toes, also stored in the boot boxes.

Any form of jewellery, except for a holy medal, was forbidden, but we could decorate our hair with bobby pins or clasps, as long as they were discreet. Often, one strand of hair would be separated from the rest, combed out, fastened with a rubber band, and finished with a navy blue ribbon. Long hair had to be worn in braids or a pony tale, likewise beribboned.

On my first day, Mum caught the tram with my sister and me, and after Cheryl had disappeared off to her by-now Standard 1 classroom, I was led into the Primers' room overlooking the verandah of what had once been an elegant old Christchurch mansion and which now housed the Primary component of the College. The Secondary school was on the other side of the impressive grey Oamaru stone convent and chapel, which sat between. The convent itself was a beautiful two storey building with white arched features, a graceful colonnaded verandah with a crenellated balcony above it, and elegant garden seats tucked into little alcoves. The gardens and beds surrounding the school were full of flowers and established trees, large statues of Mary and Jesus adorned the convent entrance, and the whole was fronted by a high, red brick wall on the street edge of a long stretch of lawn. It was an outstandingly beautiful setting.

I was a little nervous about starting school, but clearly not as upset about it as the only other new entrant that morning, a child writhing and screaming on the floor, and whose spectacular tantrum was the first thing to engage my attention, understandably, as I entered my designated classroom. Holding tightly to my mother's hand, I stood transfixed, staring at this shocking display of wildly abandoned behaviour. A very attractive young nun was also down on the floor on her knees wrestling gamely with the hysterical child, whose name I have never forgotten…Marie Green. The nun was clearly angry, a deep blush heightening her cheeks and her lips grimly compressed. She finally secured the screeching pupil in a headlock and hissed through her teeth that the mother should depart forthwith. The anguished woman did so without further bidding, and after a few more blood curdling howls, Marie subsided into a bedraggled little sobbing heap, assuming a foetal position on the floorboards. The nun regained her feet and after taking a moment to compose herself, welcomed me and Mum to Room One. Formalities over, Mum said goodbye, and I was ushered over to take my place on the mat at the front of the room with the other students, where Marie eventually joined us, small body racked by spasms of distress for some time thereafter. My gaze lingered on her. Did she know something I didn't about this institution called 'school'? If, in fact, I had known what lay ahead during the next thirteen years of my life, I'd have been down there on the floor with her, giving it heaps.

I took to school very well, considering how shy I was. I already knew a few of the children, who attended our church, or who lived near us, and I had my sister there to watch out for me, although there was no strong bond between us. We were chalk and cheese. She only had to carry out a single act of big sisterly duty that I can remember, when I wet my pants one day in the classroom. We had just returned to class after the lunch break, and I suddenly needed to urgently pass the urine I'd held in my bladder all through recess as, being a typical little kid, I didn't want to miss out on a second's play. As we knelt on the floor for the prayers that kicked off our afternoon routine, I became painfully aware that I had reached critical mass and thrust my hand into the air for permission to visit the toilet. Sister frowned and indicated with a sharp, dismissive gesture that I could wait. I bet she wished she hadn't, and her face turned puce when seconds later I burst into tears as a pungent yellow puddle formed around me on the floorboards. Cheryl was duly summoned and ordered to take me home, which displeased her no end, and as soon as we were off the school grounds she berated me severely. The bus trip home was miserable and soggy, the bus driver eyeing his ammonia-scented passenger suspiciously, and as soon as we reached our stop, Cheryl took off and left me. I eventually struggled up the driveway, sobbing and walking like an old cowhand, small legs akimbo to ease the chafing on my inner thighs, my sodden bloomers drooping around my ankles. Looking back, I can't believe that the nuns were not prepared for such an eventuality with such small children. How difficult would it have been to mop me up and put me in some spare dry knickers?

School marked the beginning of my lifetime love affair with learning, and reading in particular. I adored books and already had quite a collection. One of my fondest memories is of Mum reading to my sister and me in front of the fire on a cold winter's morning, while we ate our porridge. She read to us from the Little Golden Books collection, familiar tales like 'The Poky Little Puppy', 'Little Black Sambo' (no PC police then), 'Tootle', 'The Little Red Hen', 'The Ugly Duckling', 'Cinderella', and many others. On Sunday mornings, we listened to *Children's Hour* on the radio, and I never tired of hearing my favourite stories, like *The Three Billy Goats Gruff*, Oscar Wilde's *The Selfish Giant*, and *The Happy Prince*, or the legend of Diana and the golden apples. There was a malicious little ditty sung by Burl Ives about a group of animals living on a pond where a red snake ended up eating or scaring away the others, and I always got a vicarious thrill from that dark tale.

As soon as I learned to read myself I was unstoppable, devouring books and stories with voracious passion. I couldn't get enough, and I loved all the classics: *Through the Looking Glass*, *The Water Babies*, *Grimm's Fairy Tales*, *Hans Christian Andersen*, *Brer Rabbit*, *The Wind in the Willows*, *Tom Brown's Schooldays*. My favourites, though, were George MacDonald's *Curdie* books. A love of history was ignited, and one of my favourite books recounted the lives of courageous heroines, like Grace Darling, Joan of Arc, and Boadicea. Our parents bought us a set of Arthur Mee's children's encyclopedias, and I whiled away hours at a time feasting on all the information in those tomes. This was the beginning of my love affair with the English language and I roared through the school readers with such proficiency that I was declared a child prodigy and promptly moved up a class. In retrospect, this was not a good idea, as it meant that I was always a year younger than the others in my class all through my subsequent schooling, and only seventeen when I entered university. I was immature by nature, without having the chronological variant forced on me as well.

My first year of schooling was interrupted repeatedly by my ongoing health issues, so it was surprising that I learned to read at all, and eventually it was decided that I should have my tonsils out. The operation was performed by the family doctor at Lewisham Hospital, where I'd been born, and which was run by an order of Catholic nursing sisters of the Little Company of Mary. I was only five-years-old, so this was quite an ordeal for me to face: being away from home and family for the first time, facing fear of the unknown, and confronting terror over the invasive horror that might be involved in having an 'operation'. I was duly delivered to the hospital where I was placed in a bed in a corner of a room I shared with two elderly ladies, neither of whom appeared enamoured of the idea of having a child in close proximity. I slunk down under my covers and tried to be inconspicuous. In the morning, I was taken into surgery where I remember Doctor Shepherd placing an object that resembled a kitchen sieve over my face and following it with a foul-smelling liquid – ether, I presume – that delivered instant oblivion.

When I came to, there was no parent there to comfort me. I had to deal with intense pain in my throat and continual vomiting induced by a severe reaction to the anaesthetic. The two old ladies tut-tutted and shook their heads as the sisters tried to contain, not without some obvious impatience, my violent spasms of nausea, and there was no jelly and ice cream for me. To add insult to injury, one of the old ladies gave me a telling-off for being a rude little girl and staring at her while the doctor examined her tummy. Weak and traumatised, I was handed over to my mother after an extended stint in the geriatric ward, and delivered home in a taxi. Once home, my father took me aside and told me I had upset my mother who'd been very worried about me. Wracked with guilt, I concluded this must be why she had not visited me once in the hospital and I was ashamed to have brought such trouble on my family. My father reinforced this by saying he'd heard I showed off as I was leaving the hospital by slipping on the top step. Had I been trying to break an arm to get more attention?

Although only five, I internalised an important lesson at this point: adults as a species are beyond comprehension and totally untrustworthy. I burst into tears, stung by the injustice of these accusations, blubbering over the fact that I had not even received my promised jelly and ice cream. This elicited for me not a whit of sympathy, and I was packed off to bed with the rebuke that I really knew 'how to turn on the waterworks'.

Chapter Three

Generally speaking, I did not enjoy school. The title 'Sisters of Mercy' turned out to be a misnomer and, for the most part, the nuns gave little indication that they even *liked* children, let alone wanted to actually instruct them. Physical punishment in the form of leg slapping or being struck on the hand with a ruler was meted out for misdemeanours. Each nun wore a heavy wooden rosary around her waist, and they knew how to wield those large beads to inflict maximum pain as well. In addition, each woman wore a thick leather belt that passed through a wooden loop, something like a cinch, leaving a good length trailing down the front of the habit, and this was often used for chastisement as well. Another thick leather strap was kept rolled up in the top draw of each teacher's desk and its brandishing could turn our immature bowels to water, especially when unfurled and brought down with force on the nearest desktop, just to emphasise who had the physical power here. Each nun was a walking armoury. Milder punishment took the form of banishment to the chilly corridor. As a child who was always eager to please, I mostly escaped these assaults.

Our day always started with the same prayer, promising to do all for the glory of God. The words went something along the lines of: 'I offer you (God) my prayers, works, joys, and sufferings.' I didn't have much of a concept of suffering at this point in my life, apart from the tonsillectomy experience, and

I thought the last word was 'soft drinks'. I couldn't for the life of me understand why God wanted my soft drinks. Must get really thirsty up there in Heaven, I deduced.

After prayers, we queued up to place any pennies we'd brought from home on the outstretched palm of Black Jackie, a large, disembodied Negroid head made of cast iron and with a little lever behind one shoulder which, when pressed downwards, tipped the coins into Jackie's gaping mouth, past his lurid red lips, and down into the collection box below. The moneybox part was a truncated section of Jackie's torso, painted to resemble a black-and-white minstrel style vivid red jacket, white collar, and bowtie. (*Really* un-PC!) The money the grotesquely leering Jackie obligingly swallowed was destined for the 'missions', another nebulous concept for new entrants. Sister Theophane (we called her 'Sister Windowpane') explained that we were helping 'the black babies'. I couldn't for the life of me understand how the pennies got from Black Jackie's maw to the babies, or what they used them for, but every so often he was emptied and we tried hard to fill him up again. I just enjoyed putting the coin on his palm and propelling it into his gaping mouth. It was so mechanically neat and satisfying.

Sometimes the money never made it to Black Jackie, but was guiltily spent on a penny selection at the sweetshop on the way home.

Then it was on to lessons. There was reading, printing (making sort of crude shapes at this stage), arithmetic, religious instruction, and outdoor games. The daily programme frequently involved a trip over to the St Mary's parish church on Manchester Street. We marched along in pairs on the cinder path winding past the convent's kitchen garden, through a gate, and into the grounds of St Mary's Primary, a grim-looking red brick co-ed parish school also run by Sisters of Mercy, and regarded by us little girls as quite inferior to the College primary. My two younger brothers were destined to go to school there.

At interval, we were let loose outside for a run around, but before any exercise took place, we had to take a half-pint bottle of milk from the crates delivered to all New Zealand schools at the time to combat rickets, pellagra and other nutritional deficiencies that were the legacy of the Great Depression. I hated the milk, but there was no escape with the looming figure of an eagle-eyed nun on hand to supervise. Only when one's bottle, the contents warmed through after the obligatory couple of hours sitting in the sun, was drained, leaving the consumer feeling slightly nauseated, were we released to play. The cardboard tops of the milk bottles were collected, washed, dried, and used to make pom-poms in craft time.

In winter, we got hot cocoa, prepared by teams of volunteer mothers, and sipping the sweet, chocolatey contents of the mug was secondary to gaining precious warmth for chilled hands that wrapped gratefully around it. We had to line up along the big verandah at the front of the school building, while the mothers worked their way along the queue, pouring the cocoa from enormous aluminium teapots. If you were lucky, you might even get a top-up. The warmth delivered to one's inner core by the delicious hot liquid was soon dissipated once we were back in the freezing classroom.

New Zealand buildings of the time did not do heating well, and all our classrooms were bitterly cold in the winter months. We frequently had to interrupt our lessons to do physical exercises to get our circulation going, flinging our small arms about in all directions, and stamping chilled feet. Our family home was equally cold, with no insulation and only a small coal-burning fireplace for heating. My father was always stationed squarely in front of it to bask in the optimum heat, and if we kids encroached we were beaten away to the peripheries with a snarl. Bed was a cold refuge since there were no electric blankets then, only a hot water bottle for some short-lived comfort before it turned icy. On winter mornings, my sister and I dressed in front of a tiny cast iron two bar heater, throwing on our clothes as fast as we could to get down to the breakfast room and the fire. One morning, my sister jabbed a safety pin into one of the glowing red bars, there was a blinding flash, and thereafter we had a one bar heater.

After lunch every day, we had an unusual ritual called 'being bluebirds'. This involved folding one's arms on the desktop and resting one's head on them. The arms were the metaphorical 'nest' and our small heads the 'bluebirds'. Some kids did actually drop off, but I don't remember ever doing so. I was ever the alert flight or fright member of the herd. Following bluebird time, we were each given a rock-hard lump of plasticine and expected to make something creative. Rendering said plasticine warm, soft and malleable required much vigorous squeezing and rolling around of the unyielding lump on the desktop with the flat of one's hand. By the time you got it sufficiently pliable to work with, it was time to return it to the box. My favourite thing to make, continuing the nesting theme, was a bowl-shaped nidus crammed with eggs.

I always enjoyed art, although I had no skills in this field, helping to cover the desks with newspapers and mix the paints before getting to work on a masterpiece, which were all pretty much the same: stick figure portraits of one's pets or family, or a house with a smoking chimney, paths, fences, and flower garden. A benevolently smiling sun and a few birds were obligatory to complete the scene. If Sister decided your finished product had merit, it would be displayed on the classroom wall. Otherwise, it was hung up to dry and you got to take it home to your folks, whose praise was transparently forced before the artwork was quietly relegated to the bin. No fridge magnets, then; actually, no fridge.

If Sister Theophane judged that you had made a superior scholarly effort on any one day, you were given the privilege of playing with the enormous dolls' house, that sat in a corner at the front of the classroom, for the final half hour of the school day, an award I vied diligently for, as I adored its miniature otherworldliness.

On a fine afternoon, Sister took us outside for recreation, most of which involved ball games, tag, or group sing-songs with accompanying actions, like 'The Farmer in the Dell' and 'Punchinello Funny Fellow'. The sisters had a deserved reputation for excelling at music, so there was lots of singing, hymns mostly, folk dancing, and school productions. My class even had a little percussion band for a while. (Emulating Mrs Malaprop, I called it the 'concussion' band, which amused my parents. Actually, the din we generated could certainly give you a headache!). I longed to beat one of the little drums, or clash the cymbals, but was predictably relegated to the back row with a triangle.

When the bell rang out at three pm, we collected hats, blazers, shoes (slippers were worn in class), and bags from the cloakroom before traipsing past our teacher while she appraised each child for correctly worn uniform. Inspection completed, we proceeded out of the building, across the playground, through the big double gates, and out on to the street for the walk to the bus stop and the journey home. (Big red buses replaced the old electric trams. This mark of progress was universally acclaimed, but I missed the elegant old trams that swayed along between their mortised tracks, the overhead wires hissing and sparking). We all had pink rectangular students' bus tickets, which we presented to the driver for a puncture wound from his clippers. If the bus became crowded, we were expected to surrender our seats to adults, and did so without hesitation. The bus my sister and I caught seldom travelled as far as our street, so we endured a thirty-minute walk home from the 'terminus' every day, especially cruel on a cold wintry afternoon, or if it were raining. I frequently crawled into bed exhausted before dinner time and missed many a meal by falling instantly into a deep sleep. Then Mum woke us in the morning and we did it all over again. I always counted the days to the school holidays.

Although I longed for every weekend, they were frequently stressful rather than a time to relax. While I wanted nothing more than to curl up with a stack of books and comics, my sister insisted that every Saturday be spent at the local Century cinema to participate in the kids' afternoon matinee. The movies shown were eminently forgettable, and if the screenings involved *The Three Stooges*, which they often did, my sister would burst into tears, as she hated their physical slapstick. Cartoon parades were the most popular, and I liked Ma and Pa Kettle because they lived on a farm with lots of animals. I was passionate about animals. Anyway, I would always muster a feeble protest about spending Saturday afternoons amongst a bunch of obnoxious kids who kicked the back of your seat, yelled and yahooed, stuck chewing gum in your hair, and rolled their Jaffas down the stairs to shrieks of derision from the juvenile audience, but to no avail. My sister always had the firm backing of our mother and so it was off to the pictures, tearfully abandoning my beloved books and smarting at the indifference shown towards my own predilections. This was my training in subserving myself to others.

I was always overjoyed when we got a wet Saturday, as that precluded any trips that might cause me a soaking and jeopardise my still-fragile health. On such days, Dad would make toffee with us, one of my favourite childhood memories. Cooking distraction over, I was free to snuggle up with my books again, with the added bonus of having freshly made toffee to suck on. Sometimes, on a Saturday morning we caught the bus into the city and visited the library. Our little local bookshop had a small number of books you could borrow, but nothing like the cornucopia the city library had to offer. For a bibliophile such as I was, it was paradise. I read all Enid Blyton's *Famous Five* and *Secret Seven* series, and I loved a set of stories I found called *The Bobbsey Twins*. My idea of heaven is a beautiful library, vast and peaceful, crammed with books, doors opening to a sun-drenched garden where you can read under the trees. Maybe some toffee to be had, too.

Toffee aside, Dad's idea of a sweet treat was sometimes bizarre. He'd wrap a small piece of wood, contrived to look like a chocolate bar, in greaseproof paper and put it in your lunchbox. Of course, you'd open it with fumbling excitement only to be bitterly disappointed – not to mention angry – while your classmates fell about laughing. His sense of humour was, well, typically cruel.

Having said that, I still cling to two pleasant memories of my childhood with him. He told me that a cat's puckered little anus was called a ninepence: too big for a thruppeny bit, or even a sixpence, so hence a combined ninepence. I loved it. When I asked him why cats had a little gusset in their ears, he said that was where they kept their spare change. This appealed to my childish imagination.

Not much, but it still makes me smile.

Apart from the long summer break, school holidays of a fortnight's duration came at the end of Term One, in autumn, and at the end or Term Two in August, as winter was drawing to a close, so there was usually some pleasant weather for outings. The mums of the three families got together to organise these, and they followed a familiar pattern. We always went to the Botanical Gardens, to Abberley Park, to the Ashley River, and to Sumner Beach. Vast quantities of food, bottles of drink, and spare clothing were lugged on buses to these venues by our intrepid mothers, and there was much comparison of our respective picnic lunches to adjudicate who got the most appealing food. Cheryl and I were always wildly envious of the Radley kids who were given little jellies in sealed jars to consume. We begged Mum to follow suit, but she pooh-poohed the idea, declaring such fare 'babyish'.

Both Abberley Park and the Botanical gardens had a hollow tree, and I always made a beeline for them as soon as we arrived. Something about trees with crannies and knots excited my imagination. At school, in the playground, we had a gigantic tree that had a distinctive knot in it at small kid eye level shaped like a tiny arched doorway. I used to stare at it, willing it to swing open and reveal the puckish face of a little fairy creature peering out at me, inviting me in. My childhood imagination was always escapist, longing to be part of another world, another time, with other beings. Anywhere but where I was. As an adult, I do this now through my fantasy novels. My Irish grandmother had instilled in me a firm belief in the fairy world, and my own Irish DNA made me more than receptive to this belief.

But I began to realise, halfway through my first school year, that something was up with my mother. She had grown a big belly, and although she was now thirty-nine years old, she was clearly pregnant. I remained, however, ignorant of the biological sequiturs involved in the condition, so did not connect my father to her state of gravidity. The nuns told us that you had a baby if God chose to give you one, which was good enough for me. I often wondered what they'd do if God decided to give one of them a baby. I thought they'd probably keep it in the convent where they'd vie with each other to cuddle and pet it.

In October, Mum disappeared into Lewisham hospital for two weeks, considered an appropriate confinement period in those days, where my brother Michael was born. My sister and I were sent to stay with our Aunt Evelyn in Durham Street, at the old manse where my Irish grandmother also lived. Feisty, eccentric, the product of a hard life which included immigration to New Zealand at the age of eighteen, all alone, she provided great distraction for any kid brooding on the mysteries of existence. I especially loved her stories about growing up in Ireland and her take on the many Celtic myths, like the banshee, leprechauns, and fairies. The stories always took on an extra dimension of drama if she was sozzled with cooking sherry at the time of narration. *

Our cousin, Mary, Evelyn's daughter, also lived at the old manse. She was a stunningly attractive young woman and had a boyfriend, Ray, who took her to cabarets, which Cheryl and I considered the acme of sophistication. We loved to perch on her bed, watching her getting dressed and putting on her makeup, which voyeurism she patiently indulged. Ray would arrive wearing a tuxedo to complete the aura of brilliance surrounding their courtship, and we would watch them set off down the front path together to the waiting taxi, hands clasped to our breasts with delight, hoping such romantic glamour would also feature in our future.

Later, we were preening flower girls at Ray and Mary's wedding. They had six kids, including twins, before they eventually divorced.

After three weeks, my sister and I returned home. The extra week's absence had been allotted my mother to give her some time to adjust to life with a new baby again, minus the demands of two other children. My sister and I were anxious to meet our new baby brother, whom we had not yet seen. I'd been very homesick and was desperate to see my mother again, but there was no warm reunion, no loving embrace. Instead she seemed distant and distracted, completely focused on her new child and keeping her husband content. With three children under seven now, that husband made no allowances for the impact of her additional workload on his privileges, which he expected to be prioritised as per normal. What Mum needed was to vent her frustrations on someone. Positioned as I was, now, between the princess and the golden child, I sensed, with unerring perception, my vulnerability in this new hierarchy.

*For a more detailed account of my Irish gran, read *The Siren Sea.*

Chapter Four

The birth of my brother completely recalibrated my already shaky status within my family. My mother was besotted with him. He weighed in at ten pounds at birth, and to me he resembled nothing so much as a big slug with a permanently grumpy expression. I'd never been the favoured younger one by any stretch of the imagination. I wore my sister's hand-me-downs, my doll was a bald, plastic mass-produced Pedigree while my sister's was a custom-made bride doll with beautifully marcelled dark hair and a sweet porcelain face, my teddy bear was smaller than hers and disappeared when it began to leak sawdust, my essentially emotional nature was ridiculed, and I had never experienced that spoiled younger child feeling, ever. But now I was relegated to middle child, and while my sister took her revenge on me by gushing over the new arrival, I withdrew into a smarting, resentful bundle, plotting revenge. At five, I did not have the resources to deal with this abrupt alteration in the family hierarchy, so the hurt and bewilderment that resulted from being thus sidelined was devastating. It was at this point in my life that I experienced the real pain of differential parenting, and, assuming an additional burden, I became, with my parents' unexpressed complicity, the scapegoat for everything that was toxic in their lives and their marriage. Of course, I didn't help my cause by playing up to get attention, any attention, trivial misdemeanours really, and punishment was viciously swift in coming. My mother told me she hated me. I was only five. Desperate, I tried to ingratiate myself with my other parent.

"You used to like me, Dad. You called me Billy."

"You used to be nice," he snarled.

One of my mother's favourite sayings, when we were growing up, and as our father's behaviour became increasingly unstable, was that he 'was not like this as a young man'. That may have been true, but it was of little comfort to his traumatised children – well, this one, anyway. Looking back, and even acknowledging the risks of labelling people, I believe he was bipolar. His violent mood swings certainly indicated an affliction of this nature. Like many big extended Irish families, we have our fair share of mental illness and alcoholism.

Post-war New Zealand had a drinking culture every bit as immature and destructive as it is now, and infamously characterised by that daily frantic glut known as 'the six o'clock swill'. New Zealand pubs of the time all had males-only bars from which women were banned. If women wanted a drink, they had to go to the lounge bar. All pubs had also, by law, to close at 6pm, so men made a beeline for the nearest watering hole when their working day ended and tanked up with as much beer as their bellies could hold over the course of one feverish hour, after which they staggered home to their families and wreaked havoc on them, behind closed doors in deceptively innocent-looking suburbia. To facilitate the swill, pubs served the beer in two litre jugs, which the watchful publican and assistants, constantly ranging up and down behind the length of the bar, filled to their brims with hoses to maximise consumption (and sales) in such a tight timeframe. Cigarette smoke hung above the patrons in a noxious cloud, and the noise of their conversation could be heard a block away.

My father attended the six o'clock swill on a regular basis, and my mother would nervously watch the clock, visibly tensing as the deadline passed and she knew he would arrive home, well oiled and spoiling for a fight. His dinner steamed over a pot of simmering water on the stove, domed with a pudding bowl and ready to be served instantly when he walked in, as any delay would risk triggering his immediate wrath. We children, already fed, shrank quietly into a corner somewhere, aware of our mother's palpable tension. Some people when they drink become mellow and amiable; others become nasty and aggressive. My father fell into the latter category and was one of those people who should not drink because it releases their baseline, unsavoury nature, which is best kept dormant.

I have vivid memories of the night he arrived home and really excelled himself with a tantrum that made previous outbursts seem tame. When he learned my mother was serving him mince, he seized his dinner plate and flung the contents up and over the kitchen walls, down which the meat and gravy dripped lazily like sticky brown lava. Then he seized a carving knife and threw it at her. Thankfully, his inebriated condition spoiled his aim and the knife missed my mother, but left an ugly raised weal on the internal kitchen door, which remained there like a stigmata for years. Finally, he lashed out at my sister – I don't remember why – and chased her into the hallway where he pinned her to the wall and drew back his fist to punch her in the head. Thankfully, she ducked at the crucial moment and his fist went through the plaster instead of her face. The horror of that moment is seared into my memory, as I was hovering beside her, screaming and sobbing, begging my father to stop his rampage. I remember he made us clean up the mess he'd made, ridiculing my trembling slowness at the task, before he staggered into his bed and we retreated, feeling empty inside, to ours.

The hole in the hallway wall was quickly plastered and painted over, and although I tried not to look at the all-too-obvious lumpy scar every time I walked past it, my eyes were involuntarily drawn to this ugly memorial, just the same, and I'd feel sick to my stomach. Our mother internalised the fact that, despite his humble origins, nutritionally speaking, her husband now considered himself, as part owner of a business, of a status that precluded eating such banal fare as mince, and he was never served it again. Even now, I ensure I eat it regularly.

Looking back, I have immense pity for my mother, trapped in her marriage with young children to care for and no income of her own, like so many wives in the fifties. Religion still defined moral boundaries at this time, and the deeply patriarchal Catholic Church imposed such a firm stigma on divorce that it was not an option for abused women amongst its adherents. They just had to get on with things the best way they could. I remember how Mum envied our next-door neighbour, Kath, whenever she saw her heading off to catch the bus to town, all decked out in her finery, which usually included her neck wreathed in one of those appalling fox fur stoles complete with head, bared teeth and beady glass eyes, that women fashionably wore in those days. Mum's face would be wistful as she watched Kath strut past from her bedroom window.

"There's Kath, off to town. Of course, she has her *own* money."

Kath also had a husband who was not a drunken bully, clearly adored her, and treated her in a gentlemanly fashion. My father, on the other hand, introduced Mum to appalled people as 'Old Greasy'. As she aged, she became quite stooped and round shouldered, as if her downtrodden status were impacting on her physical stature. One night, when Dad sat down to the table with us for dinner, he pointed sneeringly to our mother, his wife, seated at the opposite end, and said, "Look at Old Greasy. She looks like a squirrel having a shit." As we sat in stunned silence, he fell about laughing. He claimed to have several mistresses as well, all of whom apparently lived in Timaru, and were named Emma Tooks, Minnie Zilch, and Zelda Greasegirdle. He took delight in telling us how they all wore 'diaphanous' nighties. He'd repeat these, what he considered humorous, tales over and over again and expect us to be amused by them. Mum endured all these puerile humiliations in stoic silence

He walked indoors one day after work, his boots shedding clay and tar with each step, and Mum said she'd just washed the floor, could he remove them, please. He did. Then he threw them both at her.

On a Saturday night, my sister and I had to traipse around to the local dairy to purchase his sports paper, but one wet, cold evening we demurred. As Dad walked past us on his way out to run the errand himself, he said to us, "You're little shits!" A kid just never gets over that kind of verbal abuse from a parent. It lodges in your soul forever.

We tried so hard to please him, make him happy, but gratitude, kindness, tenderness were not in his lexicon and we, well, me, anyway, lost interest. His birthdays and Fathers' Day were a hollow sham, with Mum desperately trying to choreograph some sincerity into the farce and failing miserably as we kids went through the motions of filial love and devotion. I felt nothing for him. I still don't. To outsiders he could be the essence of charm, and they would have refused to believe his true nature. My mother seemed to unconsciously confirm our father's schizoid personality by using two names to address him: he was either 'Howard' or 'Pat'.

Mum never aspired to any life of her own, and seemed content with her domestic role. Although she got her driver's licence, with dad's encouragement, she refused to drive, curtailing our potential for childhood outings. Never a sociable person, by any stretch, she made her family unit her sole focus, that and keeping her house of cards aloft. She didn't foster or initiate friendships and made no effort to keep in touch with people, even her long-time best friend, Nancy. She was actively inhospitable and hated to be put out by anyone or anything. As we grew older, she started going to Catholic Women's League meetings in the evening with a few other wives, always being picked up and dropped off, and sometimes they'd go for a quiet ladies' drink on a Saturday afternoon, to a local hotel. As aforementioned, women had to use the lounge bar since they were banned from the men's bar, a dreadfully sexist practice no one questioned at the time. In my early twenties, a female friend and I, both reasonably attractive young women, integrated a men-only bar and were told by the outraged patrons, in no uncertain terms, to leave. No wonder so many New Zealand girls went nuts over the Yanks when they were here during World War Two – they actually *liked* women and sought their company. Kiwi men, on the other hand, are almost all latent homosexuals who worship at the altar of their hallowed concept of 'mateship'. Aussie men are much the same.

Mum was eventually stricken with the same illness as her father, high blood pressure, but at least she had access to drugs to alleviate the symptoms. She was a very lethargic, generally morose woman, capable of just sitting slumped in a chair for long periods, and very self-righteous in her opinions, refusing to accept any notion that contradicted her own personal viewpoint. I never, ever saw her read a book or show any intellectual interest in anything. Conversations with her were restricted to a banal, superficial level, almost formulaic, and she wasn't interested in anything except covert people watching. She had no sense of humour, never got a joke, and could be derisively cruel and censorious.

Mum had a perennially martyred air and a *laissez-faire* attitude to most things, resigning herself with a shrug to whatever happened and mustering no gumption whatsoever. She put up with the symptoms of her high blood pressure for months before she went to the doctor, swallowing Aspros like candy to quell the headaches. Oddly, though, when recounting an experience she'd had, for example the time a dog bit her at the shops, she could be quite entertaining, nailing a voice inflexion, a facial expression, or body language perfectly. Even Dad, who generally did nothing to bolster her self-esteem, conceded that she could tell a story well.

Mum didn't mother, just as Dad didn't father. Neither of them ever took the trouble to get to know me, and I learned to play my role, to stay safely in character when around them.

Life went on, as is its wont. If the Saturday ritual involved enduring yet another mind-numbing example of what passed for Hollywood generated kids' entertainment in those days, Sundays were equally predictable. The Roman Catholic Church in New Zealand was at its zenith and everybody of that denomination attended Sunday Mass. Father Patrick Peyton had launched his rosary crusade with the slogan, 'The family that prays together stays together', and even in our dysfunctional family we had rosary night once a week, where we all knelt down and prayed together. At the height of the Cold War, praying for the conversion of Russia was a popular 'intention', as they were called. With all this church going and praying, I failed to see any sign of God's grace effecting change for the better in anyone, which puzzled me deeply. My father, for example, would take communion and then terrorise his family during the coming week. A damascene moment equivalent to St Paul's never eventuated.

We were all roused early of a Sunday morning and herded off to Mass at the parish church in Innes Road, Our Lady of Fatima. This was a relatively new church, and until it was built we attended St Joseph's in Papanui, presided over by a choleric Irish priest, Father Timothy. As he thundered hellfire and brimstone from the pulpit, I cowered against my mother, convinced his wrath was directed solely at me.

The parish priest at Our Lady of Fatima was also Irish, Father O'Mahoney, and although his temperament was more benign, his sermons were of such a tedious length that parishioners tried their utmost to work out which Mass was being said by his curate, Father Murphy (yes, also Irish) who favoured brevity. Father O' Mahoney knew about this, tipped off by a papist sycophant, no doubt, and deliberately fudged the schedules to outwit the manoeuvre. A collective sigh would ripple around the congregation when he strode smugly out on to the altar. This Mass would be a one-and-a-half hour one.

There was a lot of church-going in my formative years, that's for sure. A lot of church-going, praying, singing, and kneeling. I wanted to have knees like a catwalk model, with the nicely prominent patella and subtle hollow either side, but after years on those hard pews I have splay knees with faces in them. This may be attributed to heredity, of course, but I blame all the obeisance on hard, unforgiving wooden kneelers as an undeniable contributing factor.

Following Mass, we all trooped home again, our anxious mother hurrying ahead to make breakfast for us all and check on the roast she'd left in the oven. Church-going finery was exchanged for play clothes, and we hovered around our frazzled mum until dinner was announced. New Zealand cuisine at the time was still highly derivative of British food. The central element was always a large roast of some meat:

lamb, pork, beef, sometimes chicken, with roast potatoes, kumara, carrots, or swede, and a green vegetable such as peas. Rich gravy smothered everything, and if we had chicken, a fragrant stuffing was included. Roast beef was always served with freshly ground horseradish sourced from a local paddock, and Yorkshire puddings. Mint sauce accompanied the lamb roast and homemade applesauce complemented the pork. The roasted potatoes and parsnips were always sticky brown and delicious. We seldom had dessert, but, if we did, our favourite was always 'marshmallow shape', a kind of uncooked pavlova. Those roast dinners still inspire me to emulate them, and I frequently get cravings for them. Mine, though, never turn out as well as Mum's.

Our father spent the time prior to dinner guzzling from his 'half-g' (gallon), a flagon of beer collected from the pub on a Saturday to see devotees through the only day that pubs were closed. By the time Sunday dinner was served, our father was already in a belligerent mood, so we learned to eat quickly and scatter. After dinner, he retired to bed for his afternoon nap, and everyone breathed easier, while Mum laboured through the washing up on her own.

It was around this time that my parents did a frankly bizarre thing. They left the three of us, Cheryl, Michael, and me home alone one Saturday while they attended a wedding. Left in charge as the eldest, Cheryl was still only about ten-years-old. She encouraged Michael, who was only about four, to gang up on me and I found myself locked out of the house. As I grew angrier, demanding to be let back in, they both stood taunting me through the large plate glass window of the breakfast room. In a rage, I smacked it with my open palm, and to the horror of all three of us, it disintegrated in a gracefully collapsing wall of glass shards. I was only small, so I think it must have been seriously flawed somehow. I braced myself for the inevitable hiding when our parents returned, but they both said very little, Dad looking particularly grim as he cleared the mess and boarded up the empty frame. I guess they felt guilty for leaving us. I felt secretly pleased with the way I'd wiped the triumphant grins off my siblings' faces.

By this time I had reached Standard 1, and had a new teacher, Sister de Sales, a big jolly woman with spectacles, probably in her thirties, who made it immediately clear that she had a soft spot for me. The other kids called me 'teacher's pet', and I loved it, basking in the unfamiliar warmth of being someone's favourite at last. I could do no wrong, and was even appointed 'stairs monitor', permitted to wear a small badge befitting my rank and feeling quite drunk with power. I didn't have to do much for my commission, just stand on the landing and look imperious as the students trooped back to class after interval and lunch. My little cardboard badge that Sister had made for me inevitably wound up in the wash when I forgot to remove it from my uniform, and disintegrated in a pulpy mess. I resigned my prefectorial position immediately. It was nothing without the badge.

My hard-won charisma was somewhat diluted by the fact that I had broken out in a really ugly bout of 'school sores', or impetigo, which covered my entire lower jaw, oozing yellow matter and itching unbearably. Whenever a scab did manage to form, I promptly scratched it off again. My parents, reiterated by the family doctor, told me the sores were the result of my being a dirty little girl who didn't wash her hands enough, and the other kids treated me like a leper, so my hard-won hubris soon crumbled. (The 'dirty hands' accusation cut deep, and as an adult I frequently wash my hands over a day, unable to bear the thought of any contamination on them.) Sister, however, never flagged in her doting, even when the lower half of my face was a suppurating mess, so that kept me going. It was under her aegis that I was able to overcome my shyness and participate in class drama productions, which usually had a religious theme. My moment of glory came when I was given the role of the Virgin Mary in a play about the Annunciation, which we performed for the whole school. On a more secular note, I had the starring role in a dramatisation of 'Chicken Licken', that addlepated wee poltroon who thought the sky was falling on his head. A beaming Sister assured me I'd done a great job in this demanding role, and my heart swelled with pride.

However, the best was yet to come, and I was given the role of the princeling son (in an all girls school we had no choice but to reverse the Elizabethan principle of males playing females) in a school wide dramatisation of 'The Princess and the Pea', which was performed for all the students, including St Mary's Parish Primary, and at an evening show before the parents as well. I can remember wearing a little suit of gold and green satin, and my opening lines came when I was caught playing tiddlywinks behind the king's throne instead of taking an interest in a prospective wife for my future. As I recall, it was a comic take on the classic Hans Christian Andersen fairytale, and I loved hearing the spontaneous laughter from the audience. At the happy-ever-after conclusion, the princess and I performed a little minuet, centre stage, while we sang the finale song:

Lavender blue, dilly dilly
Lavender green
When I am king, dilly dilly
You shall be queen.

The applause was intoxicating.

The whole country basked in his glory when Kiwi beekeeper, Edmund Hillary, scaled Mount Everest, and I felt that maybe I, too, could get on top of this business called 'life'.

I was abruptly brought back to earth when my family attributed my burgeoning success as a thespian to my inherent trait of 'exhibitionism'. Subsequently, I was often accused of this failing, and the helpless anger and humiliation it engendered still hurt. The intervening years before I reached secondary school provided no opportunities for me to pursue any interest in the dramatic arts, and although there were major school productions during my teens, I did not audition, despite having a lovely speaking voice, contenting myself with bit parts. I no longer had any confidence in speaking or acting in front of either classmates or adults.

But I did have one final moment of glory in my last year of secondary schooling. I was chosen to be part of the school debating team for the prestigious Bishop Lyons Shield speaking competition, a prize hotly contested for by all the Catholic schools in the diocese. I found it all nerve wracking, but was determined to do my best for the school and the sweet old nun who coached us.

Not only did our team win the debate but I won the prize for Best Speaker, and we brought home the Shield. The results, including my name and award, were published in the Press and my kudos at school soared. Not at home though, where my success was brushed aside. Not one family member had even come to hear my speech.

To backtrack, riding the crest of my new wave of confidence and budding sense of self-worth, however short-lived, it was around this time that I hatched a plot to kidnap the school cat, a magnificent ginger tom called Marmalade, with whom I had struck up an affectionate relationship. I discussed this plan with Sister de Sales, and since Marmalade was a tolerated stray who had taken up residence at the convent, being fed on scraps by the kitchen sisters, she thought I may be able to adopt him, if I asked Reverend Mother for her permission. Abandoning my usual *modus operandi* of smuggling pets into the house, I actually asked my parents for permission (Sister had insisted on it) and was pleasantly surprised when they agreed. (I had nuns on my side. That had been the missing factor!). Reverend Mother gave her blessing and Marmalade was duly transported home. I was ecstatic. A pet of my own at last! Sadly, Marmalade was apparently about as keen on living with my family as I was, and promptly absconded. Weeks later I found out that he was with the Radleys, and Wendy, their daughter, whom I had known since we were babies and who attended St Mary's with me, was smug in informing me of my erstwhile pet's seizure, since they refused to return him. I was outraged, but there was nothing I could do. However, there was unspoken rivalry amongst the three families, and Dad did not like losing out to anyone, so he promptly got me another ginger cat, a young kitten. I was mollified, though it still hurt every time I saw Marmalade.

I also published my first story during this period, a personal narrative titled 'My Pet', an account of the day Dad took me to the SPCA to get my ginger tabby, Apricot, Marmalade's replacement. Sister de Sales was effusive with her praise, the story was given to Reverend Mother for her evaluation, and subsequently included in the school magazine at the end of the year. I was delighted, and a deep love of writing was born. I subsequently had many poems and stories published in the school magazine. I was a terrible romancer as a kid, making up stories both verbal and written, and sometimes getting myself into strife as a result. I made up whole sagas and told them to my sister in bed at night. I invented a whole other branch of my family who owned a vast sheep station, and promised my best friend I'd take her there for a rural holiday. Predictably, once rumbled, (my friend's parents naturally asked my parents about the planned adventure) this flair for storytelling was derided as just another flaw in my character.

Sister de Sales' passion was religious education, and while I struggled to get my head around purgatory, limbo, Hell, and trans-substantiation, it was her lessons on sin, that impressed me deeply. We were being prepared for our First Communion. She would draw three parallel circles on the board and explain that the clear, unblemished one was the soul of a virtuous person, like Our Lady, while the others, covered in chalk smears to illustrate the point, were the souls of sinners. There were two kinds of sin, she explained, venial and mortal. Venial sins were sort of petty misdemeanours, like kicking your brother, while mortal sins were biggies, really serious, and, if unrepented, consigned you to Hell. Missing Mass on a Sunday just once, unless you were ill or otherwise incapacitated, was a mortal sin. Pretty harsh, I thought. (When I was older and more cynical I realised this particular mortal sin was linked to the church's need to get a full collection plate, just as the fish on Fridays rule was linked to a papal ruse to help impoverished fishermen.) The soul with the venial sins had light little smudges on it, while on the soul with the mortal sins Sister really ground the chalk in to resemble deep, corrosive chancres of vile iniquity. I was puzzled to think that my soul was so tritely circular, perhaps tucked away in my abdomen or chest cavity. I preferred to visualise it as a sort of ectoplasmic entity that duplicated within my body the curves, contours, and extremities of my fleshly presence. Oh well, no doubt Sister knew best.

We had reached the age of reason and were being groomed for our next big Catholic milestone: the sacrament of the Eucharist. Everything we did was now preparation for this auspicious event. Collecting holy pictures was competitive, and we were immersed in the lives of the saints. We wanted to be good and we wanted to be seen to be good. At lunchtimes we were now encouraged to forfeit some playtime and make 'a visit', that is to go and pray in the convent chapel adjacent to our playground. We were only too eager to please and, about ten minutes before the bell to end lunchtime, we made quite a show of trooping into the cloakroom en masse, hoping the sisters would take note of our holiness. We donned our hats (*de rigueur* in church at the time for all women and girls), a white panama in summer, a navy blue felt in winter, and marched off to the chapel, the only part of the old school and convent that still remains. I loved the walk to the chapel, crossing the shingle driveway, passing the languorously drooping elm tree with its circular seat embracing the trunk, where nuns would sit in the evening reading their office, and into the cool, dark interior of the little Gothic building itself, tabernacle lamp glowing red, a statue of Our Lady on the altar extending welcoming arms towards us, a lingering whiff of incense from the nuns' evening Benedictions in the air. We all carried tortoiseshell rosary beads in our pockets or around our necks and these were whipped out to be thumbed in the enveloping peace of this tranquil place of prayer. The Catholic Church pre-Vatican Two really knew how to appeal to one's sensuous, romantic side.

Then it was on to making our First Confession. You could not take communion until you had made your First Confession. This was a scary prospect, as you had to go into the confessional box, an eerily silent and dark cupboard on one or the other side of the equally tenebrous closet where the priest sat, waiting to slide back a small grille, which signalled your turn to spew forth the long catalogue of sins you'd accumulated during seven years of total amorality. I opted for the customary safe list my friends and I had agreed on: bad language, lies, fighting with siblings, skipping homework, teasing other kids. Later on, we added 'impure thoughts' to the list. The priest must have been bored to death by the repetitive litanies.

Once First Confession was out of the way, we got on with prep for First Communion and were thoroughly schooled in the mysteries of the Eucharist by both Sister and one of the parish priests, Father Heagney. On the chosen Sunday morning, we attended Mass at St Mary's rather than our individual parish churches. The girls wore white dresses and veils, the boys their school uniform with the variant of white shirt and tie. All the girls carried a little mother-of-pearl bound prayer book as well. My dress was particularly beautiful, quite unexpected, and I felt like a movie star in it. I believe it was gifted to my parents by a family friend, who took pity on me for the way I always got second best. The dress originally intended for me, a limp little white lawn affair, had been loaned by the nuns. Many years later, a person I grew up with, told me that my differential treatment scandalised everyone acquainted with my family. I was shocked, as I hadn't thought anyone noticed.

Once Mass was over, the communicants were ushered into the church hall and treated to a slap-up breakfast of cereal, sausages, eggs, and toast, with a special treat of bottled fizzy drinks to wash it all down. A combination of greasy food and pop meant some unseemly piles of vomit in the church grounds afterwards, but, generally speaking, a good time was had by all, and proud parents took lots of photos of their respective offspring with their Box Brownies.

Despite all the religious indoctrination, I had a brief dalliance with theft while in Sister de Sale's class. A child brought a wonderful toy to school that had been sent to her from overseas. It was a beautiful clockwork frog and I was smitten when she demonstrated its moving parts for the class. I simply had to possess it! I waited my chance, and as soon as the opportunity presented itself, I sneaked it from her desk and hid it in mine. When the distraught child reported her missing toy, Sister shut us all in and proceeded to search every desk. Panic! I surreptitiously shoved froggy into another child's desk and upon its discovery she was subsequently blamed for the crime, tearfully protesting her innocence. I still feel shame over that cowardly act, and I never stole again, my potentially criminal career nipped in the bud.

It was also about this time that I made a foray into the esoteric world of ballet. I had no interest in ballet, but my sister had developed a passion for it, bolstered by a collection of books on the subject with titles like *Clarissa at Covent Garden*, and so I had to tag along to the Saturday morning lessons, whether I wanted to or not. I'd asked to learn the piano but been turned down. I did like the soft little pink ballet shoes, though. They appealed to my aesthetic sense very much, so light, pliable, and, well, pink – my favourite colour. We only stayed long enough to participate in one concert performed in the old Civic Theatre building, and in a neat twist of irony, the dance the teacher chose for my star turn required a tutu. So, by default, I got to wear all the white satin, tulle, and sequins, while my fuming sister was relegated to a green, floaty sea nymph costume of uneven hem length, which was hardly fetching. She canned further lessons in disgust, which meant I also had to follow suit. I was delighted, having had my moment of unexpected glory, and doing quite well despite, as my teacher pointed out, my hopelessly flat feet, which precluded any future career in the balletic arts. In short, she advised my mother not to waste any more money on lessons for me.

By way of compensation, Mum took my sister and me to see some live ballet, and, to my surprise, I really enjoyed it. A stunning performance of *Giselle*, especially the part where she goes mad, fired my imagination, and I still love an evening at the ballet.

During this period, I also went to my first circus, not having formed any firm ideas about animal exploitation at this point in my life. As we were shown to our seats in the big top in Hagley Park, we had to walk past a clown who was busily knitting, perched on a stool. As I drew abreast of him and paused to stare, he looked up, smiled, and said, "Hello. I knew you were coming tonight." Then he gave me a big wink. The impact of this simple statement, however fanciful, had me fairly floating to my seat and I have never forgotten how startlingly wonderful was the impact of that kind remark.

Sometimes, the three families got together for celebrations like birthdays and other milestones, for example, a child's baptism. As is the norm in New Zealand culture, the men all gathered in the kitchen, where they drank steadily, while the kids played outside and the women organised the setting out of food before congregating in the lounge, where someone would belt out familiar tunes on the piano. I don't remember a single party where the two sexes commingled. When the dads were well oiled, they'd often play games with us, like blind man's bluff, or walk the plank. They smelled of beer and cigarette smoke, their faces flushed and their eyes bloodshot. The party food, which eventually drew everyone together, was pretty predictable standard fare: sandwiches, sausage rolls, cheerios (little red sausages), lots of tomato sauce, and a variety of cakes, slices, and homemade biscuits. The party fare always included a cream sponge and a pavlova cake, or meringues. The custom was for each guest to 'bring a plate', that is a platter of food. Many a newcomer to Kiwi culture has interpreted that instruction quite literally and turned up with a bare plate.

When you look back on a certain incident in your childhood, the memory of which you doggedly retain, you are sometimes baffled by what prompted your behaviour. June Fogarty, a matriarch of one of the triumvirate of families threw a party for my ninth birthday, as Mum was still in the hospital after giving birth to my brother, Sean – not that she ever organised birthday parties for us, anyway, especially not for me. My father was seated next to an elderly grandfather on the settee, when I happened to glance over at him and felt an overwhelming urge to cause him pain. I crossed the room, small fists clenched, and kicked him as hard as I could in the shins. There was shocked silence, so I gave him another hefty boot. There wasn't much he could do to me in front of everyone, and I was hauled off him by a couple of guests after I sailed in for my third assault. I remember the outrage in his eyes very clearly, and I had a sensation of absolute euphoria.

Later that night, he dragged me home and locked me in the dark, spider-infested garden shed, where I languished for an hour or so, weeping quietly. On that auspicious evening, I had launched a brief, heroic rebellion, quickly crushed by superior forces but exhilarating, nonetheless. For one glorious moment the worm had turned.

My sister and I continued to enjoy periods, mostly in the school holidays, billeted with an assortment of aunts and uncles. I liked Durham Street sojourns best, staying in the old manse with Aunty Evelyn and her second husband, Arty. Her first husband, Hugh, had passed away from TB, and her daughter, our aforementioned cousin, Mary, was also afflicted by the disease, until the miracle of antimicrobials produced during the war years put an end to this ancient, fatal illness. Evelyn had a son, too, our cousin, Hugh, named for his late father, who had joined the Marist brothers at the age of fourteen. He sometimes came home for a visit while we were there, and he'd always tease me because I had trouble with his name, calling him 'Phew'. I think he joined the brothers too young, before he was really capable of making decisions about lifelong commitments. He was a total party animal and created quite a scandal when he ended up leaving the brotherhood to marry, not long before dying of a heart attack. Everybody loved him.

But it was my Irish grandmother who was the big attraction at the manse, with her stories and eccentricities, and she was the first dead person I ever saw, passing away in her nineties when I was about eight. I remember catching my breath in terror as I was propelled towards the coffin to say goodbye, but she looked so lovely and peaceful, resting on her satin pillow, not scary at all.

Uncle Arty, short for Arthur, was a good bloke with a sense of fun. He'd chase us brandishing his garden hoe and with his false teeth ghoulishly protruding between his lips, while we adored making a big production of running away, wildly screaming our mock terror. Arty told us there was a secret panel in the old house's wainscotting, and we spent hours looking for it, as well as endlessly sliding down the banisters on the imposing staircase. Aunty Evelyn and Uncle Arty liked to drink secretly in their bedroom. I have no idea why they were so clandestine about it, as we were very non-judgemental about adults drinking alcohol, having seen so much of it. I think they thought we didn't know, but grownups seem to quickly forget that kids miss nothing.

There were a couple of interesting neighbours, too, a young lad called Rowan Hook who was a little older than me and Cheryl, and a girl called Antonia, who was about the same age. Antonia's mother ran a boarding house in an old, shambling, run down two-storey place around the corner, and Antonia invited us to visit her there. Most of the boarders seemed to be young men with motorbikes, but what interested me most was Antonia's pet magpie, which chattered away like a parrot.

With Rowan we had more of a fraught relationship, and he often went off in a huff, festering for a few days before he reappeared. Uncle Arty called him the 'Hoooook boy', which amused us no end.

When Cheryl got her first pubic hair, we agreed, having recoiled in disgust, that we weren't having any of it, and while she surreptitiously lowered her knickers in a sheltered corner of the verandah one morning, I carefully snipped it off with a scissors. Sadly, this pruning only seemed to stimulate fresh growth, and we conceded defeat, my sister resigning herself to a hairy pubis, while vengefully reminding me that I was next.

Staying with Aunty Nell, Dad and Evelyn's sister, at her little worker's cottage in Stevens Street behind the gas works, was a very different experience. She smoked incessantly, even while dishing up tea, the cigarette poised precariously on the edge of her lip, and we'd cringe as a drooping finger of ash invariably dropped on to a plate we were expected to eat off, watching in dismay as she brushed it aside with a finger before plonking our dinner on after it.

Aunty Nell and her husband, Uncle Curly, were childless, and Cheryl and I quickly began to feel uncomfortable when Curly insisted we help him to feed the chickens and then, when we were at the back of the section, well away from prying eyes, he'd use the pretext of being affectionately avuncular to give us a cuddle, fingers probing dangerously near our groin area. We didn't make a fuss, but we did tell our parents, and holiday stays with Aunty Nell ended. After Curly died, we returned. Aunty Nell let us drink our tea out of her best bone china, but she also made us go to church twice on Sunday – morning Mass, evening Benediction – which we considered excessive. I loved the Catholic Basilica on Barbadoes Street, though, built in a French neo-classical style with a magnificent green copper-clad dome, colonnades, arches, and bronze and marble altar. Cousin Mary had been married there. The 2010, 2011 earthquakes have rendered it a broken shell, and I cannot bear to look at it when I pass.

The final couple in our firmament of home-stay relatives were Aunty Kath, Dad's widowed sister-in-law, possessed of a booming voice because she was going deaf, and her second husband, known simply as 'Old Man McCullough'. He was a lecherous old horse breeder with a magnificent rural property on Waimairi Road, and we quickly learned not to be caught alone with him, either. He leased land to a Chinese market gardener who kept a lovely, gentle old Clydesdale horse called Nellie, and my sister and I spent most of our time pulling up tasty clumps of grass for Nellie to champ on, or sitting at her feet while we made daisy chains to decorate her mane. She appeared to genuinely love our company. Later on, when I was older, I got a job picking peas for the Chinese grower.

By and large, I enjoyed the breaks away from home. Aunts and uncles did not generally play favourites, and there was less tension and, therefore, less anxiety.

My two years with Sister de Sales were among my happiest school memories, but that was about to change as I entered the Standards 3 and 4 domain of a nun talked about with dread in frightened whispers by kids whose elder siblings, like mine, had endured her tyrannical rule: Sister Augustine. Nickname: Gussie. Her reputation had not been exaggerated, as I was to learn, and beyond her in Forms 1 and 2, lurked the legendary Sister Rosalie who could make a kid pee her pants with one icy, gorgon stare. I comforted myself with the thought that I would still have Sister de Sales to visit with from time to time, but she abruptly left the convent.

You tried, Sister, you tried. But you were up against my family, just as I was. Thanks, anyway. I carried the lesson you taught me into my own years as a teacher: what a little kindness and encouragement can do for the kid who has no confidence or self-esteem, but so much potential.

Chapter Five

Sister Augustine was at the opposite end of the spectrum from Sister de Sales: loud, intolerant, untidy, disorganised, possessed of a mercurial disposition, and very eccentric. Rumour had it that, in her day, she had been a gifted teacher, but, alas, she had stayed too long at the chalkface and was quite old and cantankerous at this point. Perhaps to compensate for having nothing she could specifically call her own and nothing to expend her affections on, she had developed a perverse attachment to small reptiles. Her menagerie, comprising several gecko lizards and frogs, including a rare West Coast whistling frog, resided in a jumble of terrariums and aquariums at the back of the room. On a table next to their domain sat a motley collection of glass jars with perforated lids. At least once a day we were sent out on to the school's back playing field to snare flies and other insects for Gussie's pets. One was able to score much kudos with her if one returned with a good catch, which was then fed to the hungry critters by their delighted captor. About once a year, the frog would whistle, sending Gussie into raptures of delight. Sadly, one day he unexpectedly turned up his webbed toes and Gussie, convinced one of us was the assassin, gave us the silent treatment for three days while she sulked, writing our learning instructions for the day on the blackboard, and sitting slumped at her desk, the very picture of abject mourning. Lord Nelson (froggy only had one eye) was duly buried with much pomp.

Being sent to Coventry by our erstwhile teacher was bewildering enough, but preferable to Gussie's unpredictable, enraged rants, during which she sprayed copious amounts of saliva like a rabid dog, and we all pitied the poor kids in the front rows who vainly tried to take cover behind raised exercise books. She got some very peculiar bees in her bonnet, too. On one occasion, rebuking us for our collective lack of artistic creativity, she ordered us all to make 'dough models' for homework and when we expressed bewilderment she flew into a tantrum, threatening us with dire retribution if we did not present our creations the next day. Cheryl and I threw ourselves on the mercy of our mother, and she helped us to make a lily (Cheryl's) and a cat's face (mine), on which we daubed life-like colours with our paint boxes. The next day, when Gussie discovered that we were the only ones who had complied, while the rest of the kids had brought notes from perplexed parents excusing them, she was incandescent with rage and the kids in the front row got an unparalleled soaking. Cheryl and I were not too popular as, in Gussie's view, we had proved the ease of the task and the exercise was re-enforced for all for that night's homework, while we were exempt. At length, she acquired about twenty-five dough models, in which she soon lost interest, and which were abandoned to moulder quietly on a shelf at the back of the room

Gussie was also distressingly slovenly, her nun's habit liberally splattered with food stains and the large handkerchief she fumbled from one pocket no longer white but a dirty grey colour. Seated behind her desk, she often unconsciously hitched up her robes, treating us all to an unnerving display of voluminous salmon coloured bloomers.

Like many of the nuns I encountered, she could also be doggedly cruel. I remember her standing over me one day when we had Writing, practising our flowing script as opposed to Printing, with a heavy wooden ruler which she brought down mercilessly on my knuckles several times as punishment for what she considered my ill-formed letters. My sobbing had no effect, and she only let me be when it became obvious that my hand was too numb to even manage the pen.

Of course, we reported all this aberrant behaviour to our parents, but it fell on deaf ears. No criticism, implied or otherwise, of the Catholic clergy was permitted...which probably goes a long way to explaining how they got away with so much abuse and perversion.

My progress in erudition pretty much went out the window during those two years, although I became something of an expert at trapping insects, and things were not going well at home either. My mother, now forty-two years old, was pregnant again, and clearly feeling wretched about it. She confided to a friend that she 'felt ashamed' because she was 'so old'. I remember the night Dad announced to us kids that we were getting another sibling, my mother just stared straight ahead without comment, her face set and grim. Even though I was only nine, I was quickly attuned to her wretchedness.

Probably because of her age, this time there were complications and she was ordered to bed by the doctor to try and bring down her alarmingly high blood pressure and bad swelling in her lower limbs. My father, taking no responsibility as the co-author of her pregnancy and attendant health problems, promptly ordered her to get back on her puffy feet and carry out her domestic duties, especially those which involved her getting his meals out on time. She complied.

This was the period when I started self-mutilating, tearing pieces of skin and flesh off the area around my toes, where nobody could see the damage and I could conceal my stinking, pus-oozing feet. I kept this up for months. The only thing that helped me through this period was the fact, that while Sister Augustine's approach to following the curriculum was at best haphazard, she maintained a very comprehensive library of reading material in the classroom in a bookcase that ran the length of one wall. Since she didn't really favour teaching us anything, she was content to let us read for extended periods of time, and I took full advantage of it. Thus, I was able to escape from all the tension at home, where, landlocked between the crown princess and crown prince, I was frequently made the scapegoat for others' guilt and bitterness, into worlds of fable, fantasy, and adventure.

My younger brother, Sean, was born in Lewisham, renamed Calvary Hospital, like the rest of us, but this time my sister and I were able to stay at home because our widowed neighbour, Mrs Reece, took over the running of the house and minding of our other brother, now aged four. For some obscure reason, she disliked cooking in our kitchen, so she prepared our evening meal across the road in her own house, piled it all into pots, bowls, casseroles etc and then trundled the whole lot over to our place in a wheelbarrow, providing a bizarre sight for the amused neighbours. Apparently, she only had one meal in her culinary repertoire, fish pie, and after a week of the same, Dad dismissed her from her domestic duties and took over the cooking of our evening meal himself.

We only visited Mum once while she was in the hospital, and we were all barred entry. We had to talk to her while standing in the hospital driveway as she leaned out of a second storey window. Some ghastly penicillin-resistant staphylococcus infection called 'H bug' had killed eight babies in the maternity wing of the hospital in1955, and the nuns were still taking no chances a year after the outbreak. I remember looking up at her, aching for her to give me some acknowledgement, as I missed her so, but she virtually ignored me.

After the statutory two weeks of maternity convalescence, Mum returned to her delighted brood. It seemed that every time she doubtless hoped her childbearing days were over, and that she was close to getting her last child off her hands, my father exerted his control by making her pregnant again. Eventually, menopause reprieved her.

With the birth of a second brother, my role in the family deteriorated further. I was not just 'the middle child' any longer; I was well and truly buried in the mêlée, despised, humiliated, the butt of all ill humour. I had acquired a little ginger cat which I loved dearly, but after Sean was born my father waited until I had gone to school one morning and spirited it away. I was heartbroken, but this set a pattern of wanton cruelty that continued over the years. My father gave me vicious hidings on a regular basis, hurling me across his lap and pulling my pants down before he thrashed me for what were trivial transgressions. My sister was spared this violence, but he knew he could give me a hiding without my mother's censure. To add to the humiliation, he often did it in front of visitors. I was just a child, so couldn't put it into words, but I knew what he was doing was prurient. Years later, when my sister and I were teenagers, he'd lounge in our bedroom doorway on a weekend morning on the pretext of making conversation, with his pyjama flies gaping open. After he died, we found his stash of porn hidden in the garage. He held women in contempt, especially educated women.

Another time, he scooped up the dinner I was struggling through at the table, victim of a waning appetite, and dumped it on my head. While my siblings fell about laughing, he dragged me up to the bathroom and held my head under the cold tap to wash out the mess. My mother did nothing to defend me. That night she shampooed my hair properly while scolding me for irritating my father. On another occasion, I gagged when I found a huge cooked caterpillar in my silverbeet. Instead of an apology, my mother reacted with defensive rage, while my father told me if I had any manners I'd have eaten it and kept quiet. A child never forgets the sting of blatant injustice.

Sometimes, my pent up rage over these humiliations found its way out, even though I was too young to recognise it for what it was. I recall an incident that happened in the school playground one lunchtime. The bench seats we sat on to eat our lunches rested on a bed of shingle. I don't know why I did it, but I suddenly started kicking showers of small stones over the kids sitting on the bench directly opposite me. An enormous nun, Sister Adrian, Sister de Sales's replacement, bore down on me like an enraged locomotive and slapped me hard around the legs several times. I barely reacted. I didn't care.

Years later, when I was having counselling, my counsellor stood up during one particularly painful session, grabbed a large cushion and placed it in front of her body, telling me to 'go for it'. I never hesitated. I leaped up and punched, and sobbed, and swore, and punched until I fell back exhausted. I could not believe what I had just done.

Aware of my lowly status in the family hierarchy, my sister bullied me mercilessly, fully cognisant of the fact that there would be no retribution. When your own parents paint a target on you, you are fair game. If my sister had been compassionate by nature, I might have fared better. But she was not. And I did not. She nearly killed me by hitting me on the head with the heavy metal head of the old Hoover vacuum cleaner – I still have the dent in my skull – and she could lash out with her legs like a crazed stallion, delivering agonising blows to stomach and groin. Gentle by nature, I did not fare well in these encounters. No matter my age, I never had any comeback for her serrated-edged tongue.

Even the nuns noticed how little I ate and how thin I was becoming. They sent a message home, and the selected stratagem became that, at lunchtimes, I was not allowed to go and play until I had finished the contents of my lunchbox. Of course, I could not force the food down and so I missed many a playtime, sitting alone, feeling miserable. One reason this forced isolation was particularly upsetting was because it was during lunch that we indulged our passion for 'crazes', which changed regularly. Cats cradle was really popular for a while, and the kids who were really good at it tutored the less creative. Then knuckle bones took over, and every kid had a box of 'swaps' as well, shiny little cards and pictures which you could buy by the sheet in a stationers. Marbles were popular, too, and after the Soviets launched sputnik we went crazy over a tiny plastic version sold in dairies and filled with sweets. At home my sister and I spent hours with cut-out paper dolls that came with a variety of colourful paper clothing you could use to dress them up by folding back the little tabs around their edges. We loved our walkie-talkie dolls, too. They were the cheapest version with painted on hair, but we adored them just the same. Their eyes opened and closed, their legs were jointed, and when you tipped them over they cried, 'Mama.'

Our brother had a collection of Matchbox cars with which he played for hours. I made hats for them from the button box and the cars became customers of my hat shop, a girlish contribution my good-natured brother happily tolerated. Some of the little vehicles had names. I recall a small blue tractor named 'Zephy Madder'. I learned quickly that playing with my brother earned me Mum's approval.

We won a small doll's house in a school raffle and had endless pleasure from that, too. There was always some way to amuse ourselves, but, mostly, we loved to play outdoors; skipping, backyard cricket, riding our bikes were all favourite pastimes. An old boat provided lots of fun, too. The concrete it rested on was the 'sea', and we had a variety of weapons on board, including an old Lee Enfield rifle. Michael had a Davy Crocket hat and we recreated the movie *Davy Crocket and the River Pirates* in that little boat, alternatively shooting at the bad guys or paddling like mad to escape them. Later on, hula hoops became wildly popular. We certainly got tons of exercise.

Every year, Mum took us to the A&P show, 'when the country comes to town', and I adored visiting all the livestock pens with the sheep, cattle, and pigs, as well as spending time in the building that housed the dog show. We always got candyfloss, a dolly on a stick and a ride on the merry-go-round. The first time I went as a very young child, I slipped away from my family and got lost, ending up in the police tent and having my name announced over the PA system as a 'lost child'. One year, I won a lovely plaster dog playing the ball-in-the-clown's-mouth game. That was an unexpected thrill, one that surprised the whole family. The dog got rather dusty on our bedroom shelf, and when I attempted to wash it, it disintegrated.

The Industries Fair came to town once a year also, but that was more of an adventure to share with your friends when you were old enough to go out without adult supervision. Eating hot dogs, riding the ferris wheel, and going through the Haunted House were the obligatory rites of passage at that venue. Nobody cared about the industrial displays.

By this time, my young brother, Michael, had started school, attending the co-ed St Mary's primary School on Manchester Street behind the convent, commuting each day with his two sisters. He suffered from a weakness in his bowels and bladder and consequently sometimes soiled himself. When he reached adulthood, he was diagnosed with serious kidney disease that had been missed during his childhood by our family doctor. His unassailable status as the apple of Mum's eye did not shield him from our father's wrath on this occasion, and he was often forced to sit outside in the cold with a bucket of water and a scrubbing brush to clean his offending undies, tears trickling down his little face, while our distraught, mother observed him from the kitchen window, wringing her hands and fighting back her own tears. I've often wondered how our father felt when my brother's illness was revealed. Did he feel remorse, shame? I doubt it.

One night, Michael felt ill, and, as a child is wont to do, instead of making for bathroom or toilet, he traipsed up to our parents' room to inform them of his condition, depositing steaming little piles of vomit along the way. While Mum was trying to console her son, take care of his need, and clean up the mess, Dad followed her into the washhouse loudly lamenting the injustice that had seen his sleep disturbed. In what was to be only the second time I ever witnessed her standing up to him – I'd got up to see what all the commotion was about – my frazzled mother whipped around and said, "The trouble with you, is you shouldn't have had children!" His face morphed into something particularly ugly and he kicked her so hard I don't know how she stayed on her feet. Incidents like this, left me feeling empty inside, and our home had a hollowed out, inhospitable feeling for days afterwards.

In retrospect, my father seemed to have a love/hate relationship with my mother, and frequently made her feel guilty about her dependence on him and the fact that he had to work to provide for us all. His career choice was his, however, and he was lucky enough to be his own boss, enjoying the perks that went with that status. Working outdoors in all weather was not easy, but I never saw a man better wrapped up against the cold than he was. He always looked after number one. For example, he had a heated pad on his side of the bed for cold nights, while Mum shivered on her side. Things like that didn't bother him at all.

He'd fallen out with his partner and taken over the asphalting business on his own, putting his family through a rocky period behaviour-wise. His friendships always staled, since he tired of people just as he did pets, and worked up feverish hates against them. My sister has inherited this unfortunate trait, her most outstanding victim being her mother-in-law.

Dad's conscience would sometimes get the better of him after a particularly nasty episode with Mum, and he'd make a grand gesture to salve it, buying her something expensive, which she would accept with a martyred air. I don't think she gave him much support during times when business was slow, in mid-winter, for example, and he aware that he had bills to pay and six mouths to feed. Mum was not the empathetic type, not a person you could discuss worries or personal problems with. She was too self-centred. Dad abused the business when it suited him, though. He'd refuse to take phone calls from prospective customers in the evening, but if we kids chatted too long to friends he'd burst in angrily, ranting about it being a 'business phone'. He was alarmingly irrational.

As my sister and I grew older and enjoyed dressing up to go out, he'd look us over and declare nether of us could compete with our mother for good looks when she was young, which was nice for Mum, while doing nothing for our self-esteem. Only Dad could give a compliment at someone else's expense. Mum was certainly attractive when she was younger, but she aged badly, becoming frumpy and coarse of body very early on. Her features had assumed that rigid look of disillusionment that characterises so many women who have been married a certain length of time. In her sixties, she became quite obese. I don't think Dad's nostalgia for her youthful good looks made her feel any better about herself. Photos of Dad as a young man made me wonder what she ever saw in him: weedy, balding, and clearly revealing his self-absorption with the way he posed for the camera. Mum clearly disliked her body, and I didn't know how to help her with that. She had huge, pendulous breasts, which she hated, a strangely flat bottom for a woman, and a large protruding stomach she blamed on childbirth. I wish I could have helped her, and then perhaps she would not have projected her self-loathing on to me.

By the end of my second, and, thankfully, final year with Sister Augustine, she decided that, because I was quiet and introverted, I was thick and needed to be kept back a year, especially since I was the youngest in my level, anyway. She summoned my mother and announced her verdict. I was distraught at the idea of being held back while all my friends moved on, and my mother showed her support for me by deferring to Gussie and refusing to speak to me.

Seeing my obvious misery as the year drew to a close, Gussie relented and declared I could move up after all. Thus, I was spared another year of trapping insects and learning nothing.

I hadn't always been shy and retiring in Gussie's class, though. During one wet afternoon where we were invited to perform some distraction for the class, for some obscure reason I got up when it was my turn and impersonated a dithery old doctor who muddled through a lecture he was trying to deliver to his class at medical school, making lots of funny mistakes and getting annoyed with his worst student whom I named Hartley. My adopted persona was 'Doctor Smith'. The kids loved it, and I was frequently obliged to repeat the performance, extemporising the whole show.

Gussie even invited Mum to one of my 'shows', but she put me off my stride well and truly, sitting there with a censorious expression on her face, and it was not one of my better performances.

Probably stretching it, but perhaps this was the spark of what could have been ignited into a career as a stand-up comedian, but as with all my efforts to be noticed as a human being, my show-time career, like my acting career, was ruthlessly crushed by my parents, led by my father after Mum had reported back, and dismissed as more 'showing off'. Whenever I raised my head above the parapet, I was 'showing off". Spontaneity, wit, inventiveness...none of that cult of personality here, was the firm message. I withdrew into shameful obscurity, retreating into my own private little gulag, self-confidence eroded yet again.

Sublimating my need for affection, I'd sometimes deliberately make a fool of myself in front of my family, to get them to laugh at me, because even scorn and derision were better than no attention at all. I'd make up little rhymes and ditties and chant them off in front of them, but they were never laughing with me; they were always laughing at me. I continued to do that with people for a long time: put myself down, abase myself, and then hate myself afterwards.

Chapter Six

Because of her terrifying reputation, I was thoroughly intimidated by the prospect of entering Sister Rosalie's lair for my Standard 5 and Standard 6 education, my final Primary School years. We had all observed the tension between her and Sister Augustine and knew it stemmed from Rosie's (we gave all the nuns innocuous nicknames) awareness that graduates of Gussie's classes were sadly not up to speed with the curriculum, and that she, Rosie, would have to fill in the gaps as well as teaching the new levels, thus adding to her burden. Like all the nuns, she had an intuitive dislike of youngsters, which exacerbated her already spiteful disposition. Looking back, I'd guess she was probably in her sixties and overdue for retirement.

The shortage of teaching nuns in the Mercy order meant that we were always doubled up in our classes, the sisters having to deal with jam-packed classes of two levels at once. This did nothing to improve their temperaments. Sister Rosalie had about fifty students to teach, which fact probably went a long way to explain her ruthless approach to discipline in order to stay in control of her pre-teen, restless brood, who daily strained at the leash. There were incidents of mutiny, and while the rest of us froze in horror, the offender would be made either to stand at her desk for long, shameful periods, be cast out into the cold corridor, or, most dreaded of all, strapped on the hand. Sister Rosalie could bring that strap down on a kid's desk lid with such force that it left a white mark on the dark-stained wooden surface.

What appalled me most about all this violence, though, was the complete dearth of any semblance to Christian values, the values we had rammed down our throats on a daily basis. The kids who were pets, usually because they came from well-to-do families, were safe, but others, who lacked this immunity, especially those clearly from poor families, were singled out for cruel treatment on a regular basis. But Rosie was capricious by nature, and no one was completely safe in her domain.

I remember one incident in particular. Our desks were lined up together in pairs, each pair consisting of a Standard 5 girl seated next to a Standard 6 girl. They were the old fashioned desks with the flip-up seats and little porcelain inkwells in the lids. We used pencils for most of our work, but any essays had to be written in ink, using brightly coloured wooden pens with detachable nibs. The nibs only lasted so long before the split tips splayed out, probably from pressing too hard, and had to be replaced. Most of us used the school-provided ink, but some kids had their own bottles. Ink accidents were frequent, and messy incurring Rosie's wrath. Handwriting was one of the categories on our school reports and skilful execution was taken seriously, with awards given for the best script. God help you if you had blobs or cross-outs. God help you if you kept a messy desk, too. The interior of one's assigned desk had to be maintained in good order, and there were regular clean-outs and inspections.

One of the most harrowing parts of the school day would occur when Sister Rosalie made her rounds, aisle by aisle, to check the work in our exercise books, which we had to have ready, open on our desks. There was a row of single desks along the windows side of the classroom, and then the double row I was in, so it was down our aisle that she always came first. She carried out her inspection of the windows row girls, and then, now at the back of the room, began working her way up towards the front of the row I was in, about a third of the way along. Without comment, she flicked through the pages of my book, and then looked over at the book of my companion, leaning slightly across my desk as she did so. "What's that?" she asked abruptly, stabbing with a finger, and, because I was only eleven years old and naturally curious, I reflexively swivelled my head towards my fellow student's book, a Pavlovian response, you could say. I never saw Sister move, but the next instant she drove her closed fist into the side of my head, the soft part of my temple just behind my right eye. I didn't make a sound. I was too shocked and in too much pain to react. "Keep your eyes on your own work!" she snarled to accompany the blow. Then she moved on. I was still seeing stars for a long time afterwards, and, of course, the tears flowed, adding to my humiliation in front of my fellow students. Later, she gave me a look of semi-defiant pity. To this day, I remember quite clearly the feelings of grief, anger, and bewilderment engendered by the injustice of that cruel blow. There was no point in telling my parents of the incident. I knew by now that I had no worth, no value whatsoever in my family. In short, nobody cared.

When she wasn't being psychotic, Rosie was actually a good teacher. She loved Literacy, especially the mechanics of language, and it is to her that I owe my deep knowledge of the intricacies of English grammar, a skill that has been of immense value to me, both as a scholar and a writer. While I excelled at English and other literary subjects, I struggled with maths. I did at least commit my times tables to memory, though, because we had to chant them through every day in rote fashion as Rosie marched up and down, keeping the rhythm going by waving a yard ruler about like a malevolent human metronome.

Once a week, an extremely handsome young priest came to our class to lecture us about the more esoteric punctilios of the Catholic faith. His name was Father Deans and we always nudged each other, tittering quietly, when we noted how Rosie blushed whenever he came into the room. He was visibly terribly conflicted, even to our childish eyes, his face pale, his eyes red-rimmed, fiddling nervously with a matchbox as he tried to focus on his instruction. If we saw him outside in the grounds, he was always smoking, pacing up and down like a caged lion, his inner turmoil all too obvious. One day, he did not appear, and none of us was surprised to learn that he had left the priesthood. His replacement was a hoary, snuffly old priest, and Rosie no longer blushed.

On Thursday afternoons we played netball in Hagley Park, and although I was always in a bottom team, not having a sporty bone in my body, I enjoyed the break from the oppressive atmosphere in the classroom. In Standard 6, or Form 11, as it was known, we got to go to cooking every Monday afternoon at the Normal School (!) in Kilmore Street, where we concocted such gourmet delicacies as boiled carrots in white sauce, fried liver, and apple crumble. We wore white aprons and white housemaid-style caps with our names embroidered on them, and each girl worked at her own little well equipped station under the watchful eye of the Home Economics teacher, who seemed to like kids more than the nuns did. My favourite part of this schedule was calling in to the Victoria Street pet shop on the way home. I loved all animals with a passion, but especially cats and dogs and there were always kittens and puppies to cuddle.

About this time, I was also introduced to the bizarre world of orthodontics. I had quite a large gap between my two front teeth, and the school dental nurse service had sent a letter to my parents recommending I be fitted with a dental plate to pull my teeth together. I was duly handed over to an orthodontist with a good reputation, Mr Donaldson, who ran his clinic from the prestigious Harley Building on Cambridge Terrace in the central city. He made a mould out of a gooey, offensive tasting substance he crammed into my mouth and subsequently fitted me with a sinister looking contraption that sprouted wires in variously tortured configurations, and which I promptly dubbed 'crabby'.

I hated crabby. A couple of other kids I knew had dental plates, but they were made out of a pretty pink semi-transparent material resembling bubble gum, much more attractive than my clunky, ochre coloured specimen that resembled a bloated tick. I set about plotting crabby's demise. I abandoned him on the front porch of the school where he was found and returned to me with annoying speed. I lost him at Hagley Park amongst the autumn leaves. I left mark two in my uniform pocket when I dumped it into the washing machine for its weekly wash and he went through the wringer with predictable results. Mark three met an untimely death under the wheels of Dad's truck. By this time, my exasperated parents, not to mention the increasingly twitchy Mr Donaldson, decided my teeth looked good enough, and my fling with cosmetic dentistry ended, to my great relief. Mr Donaldson's Parthian shot was that he'd known all along that I wasn't wearing crabby when I claimed I was, and that I was a mendacious little brat destined for perdition.

Years later, while studying at University, I learned that in the Middle Ages people believed a gap-toothed woman was a nymphomaniac. It seems my career as a wanton harlot had been nipped in the bud.

Escaping from Mr Donaldson did not exempt me from the horrors of school dentistry, though. St Mary's was located alongside the dental nurses' training school in an old mansion called Hollylea, and we provided the fodder for the practical component of their study. Our perfectly healthy young second teeth, with no signs of decay, were mercilessly drilled into and refilled with black mercury amalgam. They effectively destroyed the teeth, and in many cases the health, of the baby boomer generation, and nobody stopped them, not the parents, not our teachers, not the medical profession; nobody. It was a shocking abuse of bureaucratic privilege.

Another preoccupation of my young years was pets. Having no bond to speak of with any significant adult, I expended my love on animals. For a while I had a little green budgie, but in what would become a cruel and hurtful pattern, my father got rid of Greenie while I was at school one day. While we were growing up he always kept canaries, although it was Mum who did all the hard work, cleaning cages, feeding and watering them. Nobody dared question his right to have pets.

My persistent pleadings to have a cat were finally successful when I got a small ginger kitten from the SPCA. This was my beloved Apricot, who likewise disappeared one day just before Sean was born on the pretext that you couldn't have a cat with a baby. Undeterred by the pain, I went underground and attempted to smuggle various pets home, getting myself in a lot of strife with my enraged father in the process. Finally, all my cajolery and subterfuge paid off and we got a beautiful little miniature dachshund puppy, Heidi, the love of my life. Mum, the real person the dog had been acquired for in one of my father's guilt-trip phases, got rid of her by overfeeding her, and she died of a heart attack aged only seven years, sparing her the anticipated disappearing act. There were two more painful pet episodes to come. All in good time. I promised myself that when I had my own place I'd have as many pets as I could feasibly cram into it.

After two years of misery and tension in Rosie's class, I moved on to my secondary education with 'the big girls'. I opted for the Professional course (academic) as opposed to the Commercial course (secretarial), which my sister chose. Badly lacking in confidence, still shy, deeply innocent, and totally not-at-home in the world. I started my high school tuition at the age of twelve.

Chapter Seven

Secondary school at St Mary's suited me much better. I was delighted beyond words to be learning French and Latin, studying Shakespeare and classics like *Silas Marner* or *Jane Eyre*, while the nuns, in particular our Form Teacher, Sister Gemma, seemed to be more kindly disposed towards adolescent girls in their care. I had well-established friendships and made new ones as Catholic girls from various parish primary schools swelled the ranks. The old greystone Gothic buildings, though still freezing, and spreading lawns with mature trees created an atmosphere of hallowed academia, which I revelled in. Though I still struggled with Maths, I was competent in Science and did well, as always, in the literary subjects, topping the Diocese in Latin in my Third Form year. In so many ways, I was still a naïve kid, and when I turned thirteen I was the only one in the class who still didn't have her period. The nuns continued to fret over my weight, too, and I was obliged to traipse over to the convent every lunchtime to collect a mug of hot soup that was somehow meant to plump me up. The school gardener, an odd little punch drunk ex boxer, used to join me.

A group of my classmates formed a cycling club called 'Paddy's Pedal Pushers'. We thought we were very clever with our chosen title, since we literally pushed on our pedals while cycling, and pedal pushers, in the form of knee-high pants, eminently suited to cycling, were all the rage. The

'Paddy' part stemmed from the fact that we made our first sortie into the countryside on a St Patrick's Day, an annual holiday from school at the time for all Catholic students, provided it fell on a weekday. We went all over the place, including to the beach in summer, and for lunch we always lit a fire and cooked potatoes in the ashes, smearing them with butter before we devoured them, charred bits and all. We had no helmets or other sophisticated biking gear, but we always felt safe on the roads. Sometimes we left our bikes behind and took the train to Lyttelton, walking around to the old gun emplacement on Ripa Island, or taking the ferry over to Diamond Harbour to swim and relax. Setting off on a journey somewhere, savouring the anticipation of how it may unfold, has always evoked deep satisfaction and a rush of happiness for me my whole life. The physical pilgrimage is a reflection of and adjunct to the spiritual one.

I loved hanging out with my friends, especially if it meant getting away from the tensions at home for a while. We enjoyed listening to our 45s of contemporary songs, and decorated our bedroom walls with pin-ups of our favourite singers, in my case, Cliff Richards, Fabian, Bobby Rydell, John Leyton, and the Beatles of course. When TV arrived we took a while to acquire one, so I'd cycle to a friend's place one evening a week to watch 'The Beverley Hillbillies' followed by 'Doctor Kildare'. We also enjoyed swimming at the Centennial Pool and buying fish and chips to devour afterwards.

Sometimes, we'd attend a dance at a church hall, but I never really enjoyed them. The boys congregated around the door, while the girls eyed them hopefully, sitting on benches ranged along the wall like the proverbial flowers. The twist was all the rage and I just felt silly doing it and getting sore soles to my feet after a while. When we reached Sixth Form, we were eligible to attend the annual St Bedes Ball, and had to endure dancing lessons for weeks beforehand, learning how to fox trot, waltz, and do something called The Gay Gordons (!). My partner at this occasion, which had all my friends in a hormonal frenzy I failed to relate to, was a quiet lad called John. Under the watchful eyes of the priests, we worked our way through all the dances, ate supper, posed for a group photo, and, thankfully, it was all over by 11 p.m. Never a social butterfly, I couldn't wait to get away. In my Seventh Form year, I was the only girl in the class who didn't attend.

Looking back, I am impressed by how innocent and naïve we all were.

While school ticked along without drama, life in Christchurch in the Swinging 60's chugged along happily. Rock and roll was very popular, and we had our own home grown version of Elvis in the form of Johnny Devlin. We all listened to the hit parade every week and argued about the ratings the next day. There was no TV, but we had our favourite radio programmes, like *Life With Dexter*, *Night Beat With Randy Stone*, John Maybury's *The Quiz Kids* and *Lux Money Go Round*, *The Hit Parade*, and *Sunday Requests*. Our family radio occupied a small alcove in our breakfast room, and we all huddled over it of an evening, arguing over who wanted to listen to what. Parents had the final say. We all had to listen to *It's In The Bag* with Selwyn Toogood, a very popular game show that later migrated to TV. I was never mainstream in any of my tastes, and was regarded as a bit of a weirdo by my peers.

Like all good Kiwis, we worshipped at the altar of Rugby Union, and if an All Blacks game was being broadcast the whole house came to a standstill while it played out, the noise of radios turned up loudly and sports commentator Winston McCarthy's distinctive voice reverberating across the entire neighbourhood. If our team lost, you could guarantee an explosion of domestic violence that night.

For the girls, the popular game was netball, and most of my friends were mad about it. Not me, though. I would rather have watched paint dry, and I have never bought into the Kiwi obsession with sport. Now, in my sunset years, I find I have fewer bone and joint problems than my peers.

Going to the movies was still a special occasion, and now that my sister and I were older, Mum often took us to the local suburban cinema of an evening to watch movies like, *Gone With The Wind*, *The Three Faces Of Eve*, *A Town Like Alice*, *Roman Holiday*, *My Sister Eileen*, *Rebecca*, and lots of musicals, including *Guys and Dolls*, *Seven Brides For Seven Brothers* and *Singin' In The Rain*. We loved them all. The theatre manager greeted patrons at the big double glass doors marking the theatre entrance, and he was always resplendent in a tuxedo. Before the main feature, you had the 'shorts', comprising newsreels and trailers for coming attractions, and sometimes a cartoon. Then there was 'interval' during which you purchased ice creams from young lads who wandered up and down the aisles with glass-fronted boxes displaying rows of the confectionary and supported on straps over their shoulders. The ice creams were always frozen rock solid, the first bite delivering a painful stab to the forehead area.

Christchurch's city centre was dotted with movie theatres, the most prestigious being the aforementioned Regent in the Square. Its domed ceiling lit up to resemble the night sky, studded with glittering constellations when the lights went down. Two other theatres in the Square, the Tivoli and Crystal Palace, however, were of dubious reputation. Showing only B grade movies, they were referred to as 'flea pits', and nice girls did not go there, unless they wanted to be groped by unsavoury types. Everyone stood up for 'God Save The Queen' before the film commenced, and the screen was only revealed when the elaborate curtains were swept to the sides, or pleated up.

There was virtually no crime, and people left their doors unlocked if they went out. Everyone was employed, mothers stayed home with their kids, cooked, cleaned, and sewed, while fathers earned the daily bread. Everybody went to a church of some denomination on a Sunday before consuming a huge roast meal for midday dinner and then spending the rest of the day in a postprandial torpor. Nobody mowed lawns or worked around their place on a Sunday as it was considered bad form. Their neighbours would have been scandalised, even irreligious ones. All shops closed on the weekend except for movie theatres and dairies, and shops in the Brighton suburb, which had a special dispensation to open on Saturdays. It was a peaceful, predictable, narrow world in which each person knew his or her place and followed the strict social norms.

There were some renegades, though. After the James Dean/Natalie Wood movie, *Rebel Without a Cause*, became such a hit, the word 'teenager' had come to be bandied about and some began to assert themselves in the form of angst-ridden teen subcultures, to the adults' disdain. Through the media, American culture became wildly popular, and we readily adopted the new slang, using words like 'cool', 'square', and 'dig it'. Drinking Coca Cola was *de rigueur*.

We had British inspired 'teddy boys' with stovepipe trousers, 'winkle picker' shoes and duck tail quiffs, as well as 'bodgies', and 'widgies', their female counterparts, who were a uniquely Kiwi phenomenon. The widgies followed their own particular dress code, including peroxided hair, heavy eye makeup and pale pink lipstick, giving them a sexualised aura condemned by decent citizens. Bodgies and widgies hung out in selected milk bars deemed seedy by disapproving elders, but wickedly alluring for impressionable youth.

Young men souped up old cars and drove them round and round the Square, the city's central hub, picking up girls and revving their engines, the prototypes of today's 'boy racers'. When a girl in our class dyed her hair blonde, an indication that she was embracing the widgie lifestyle, the nuns were horrified and she was expelled.

Sometimes, on a Sunday, we went on a family picnic, especially during the warm summer weather. Mum would pack up a cardboard box full of sandwiches, cake, fruit, and soft drinks, and, of course the thermette was always included for boiling water for the adults' cup of tea. Ashley Gorge was a favourite venue, and we kids loved chucking stones in the river, or going on a bush walk. There was always a swimming hole available for a dip. Often, it was dark by the time we got home and everyone had to help with unloading the car. (We got a little station wagon when I was about ten. We thought she was a thing of beauty).

It was about this time, too, that a wine and dine restaurant opened up in Christchurch, a real pioneer in a city that had a dearth of fine dining facilities. It was called the Malando, and my father decided we should go there as a family, since the business was doing quite nicely at this particular point in time and he was feeling generous. He was also feeling pretentious and embarrassing. While I enjoyed the dining out experience, I cringed when my father tried to make out he was a wine snob, lingering over the cork proffered by the waiter, holding it to his nose and sniffing delicately. Then came the swirling of the thimble full of wine in the glass, more sniffing and holding of said glass up to the light, while the rest of us squirmed and tried not to catch each other's eye. In truth, he wouldn't have known a decent wine from a rancid one. If he had just been true to himself we would not have thought any the less of him, but I think Dad always aspired to be something he was not, a plutocratic, sophisticated businessman and connoisseur of fine things. He applied the same fake affectations to music appreciation, which did not alter the fact that he was utterly crude and plebeian in his true tastes and fooled no one, especially not his own family.

Anyway, he invariably ruined the dining out experience when, as the evening wound down, he realised he had to foot the bill and his mood changed to one of sullen resentment. He took up fly-fishing to get away from us, and his absences breathed an air of relaxation and serenity into our home where his presence generated a veritable miasma of tension.

Looking back, I realise what good kids we were, kids any parent should have been proud of, and for me my father's greatest fault was that he did not appreciate this fact. One of the most hurtful things he said to me was, "Don't bother me if you have any problems. I don't want to know about them." Biologically my father...and that's where it ended.

Holidays are another fond memory... well, mostly. When Cheryl and I were very young, we seemed to have holidays very close to home. I recall summer sojourns at Brooklands lagoon, and also at Brighton Beach, just a stone's throw from our own suburb. The beach at Brooklands didn't appeal to me very much because it was covered with sea snails, but I loved Brighton with its distinctive sandhills, the sand so hot under your feet you had to pronk across it like a gazelle to get to the water, and the way it was so lovely to snuggle into when you emerged chilled from your swim. There was no such thing as 'sunblock', and we often burned under the harsh New Zealand sun, skin subsequently peeling off in papery strips. Indeed, the usual practice was to smother kids with coconut oil, which pretty much basted you like a chook on a spit! Following a swim, our favourite treat was a chocolate bomb ice cream, and later on a TT2, a frozen drink on a stick.

I don't remember Mum ever swimming with us, but Dad did. At one point, in response to Dad's nagging, I think, she did actually purchase a bathing suit, an enormous blue satin contraption that ruthlessly exposed every bulge and channelled her large breasts into terrifyingly sharp cones. There is a photo of her skulking in the sandhills and glaring at the cameraman, presumably my father. The bathing suit remained unchristened and disappeared.

Through a friend, Dad made contact with a widow in Picton, Mrs Wooding, who was keen to make some money renting her house out. Picton was where my parents spent their honeymoon, so I guess it held nostalgia for them. Mrs Wooding went off to Wellington for a fortnight to stay with a daughter and we set off to sojourn in her home, usually the first couple of weeks in January. Dad insisted we leave at 5.30 in the morning 'to avoid traffic'…even though there were few vehicles on the roads in those days. Poor Mum had to wake us, still half asleep and groggy, get us fed, make sure we'd packed all necessities, load it all into the car along with us, and make sure the house was secure. Dad, meanwhile, strode around giving orders. Then off we went, and I cowered in the back dreading what lay ahead: travel sickness, on an epic scale. It usually kicked in when we hit the Hundalee, a twisty, winding, hilly road taking about an hour to climb and descend, and which Dad insisted on tackling like a deranged racing car driver, swinging violently around the bends like one possessed. As I vomited gaily into my bucket, my mother snarled at me for 'showing off.' Pretty desperate method of drawing attention to yourself! Putting me in the front of the car may have helped, but that privileged spot was reserved for my brother, Michael, who sat on Mum's lap. No child restraints or seat belts back then.

Sometimes, Dad would stop at a pub, and leave us all to swelter in the car while he lounged in the blokes' bar drinking beer and chatting to the locals. He'd bring us kids out glasses of pub raspberry and a shandy for mum. I always guzzled mine down knowing full well it would re-emerge at some later point. Then it was back on the road again, with a boozed up driver (no breathalysers then). Once, we kids had a bit of a childish bicker in the back and Dad went ape, planted his foot on the accelerator, and careered dangerously along the highway with all of us, including Mum, screaming hysterically and begging him to slow down. Ah, those were the days: vomit and adrenaline.

Once we reached our destination, Dad would disappear with the first local he was able to buddy up with and that's the last we'd see of him. Mum grimly carried on with the same routine she followed at home, and we kids ran wild exploring our new environs and doing our own thing. Mrs Wooding's house was a stately old bungalow on a cliff top overlooking Picton Harbour. The setting included a lovely terraced garden, steep winding driveway shaded by tall trees, and a quaint summerhouse. The bridge leading across to Shelly Beach was a stone's throw away, and we loved racing each other across it. I had a bright red pair of the new craze, plastic sandals, and thought I was so cool because you could wear them into the sea. Cheryl and I told Michael that the beer bottles bobbing in the water were 'bottlefish' and he subsequently spent many an hour fishing from the bridge, trying to hook one on a line baited with cheese and biscuit, the only thing they liked to eat, we assured him.

Picton was a great holiday venue. We had the foreshore a short walk away, and Shelley beach for swimming. There were boat tours of the Sounds' beauty spots to enjoy, aboard Captain Kenny's iconic *Friendship*. Fishing expeditions were so cheap the whole family could go, hauling in huge numbers of cod to take home for tea. I proved a total Jonah at fishing, catching nothing, while everyone else hauled in groaning lines with three or more fish on them. In the end, my father sneaked a couple of dead fish on to my line, and although I knew very well what he'd done, I performed the mandatory exclamations of delight.

We had several holidays in Picton and later on we vacationed in Kaikoura and Hanmer Springs as well. Nobody could go to Hanmer Springs without having a dip in the famous hot pools, but the prospect filled me with dread. You had to go in with no togs on, in your birthday suit! Of course, men and women were segregated, but even so! Bounding into a pool in front of everyone in the nick? No way! I refused. My mother and sister roasted me and I caved in. It was a hideous experience. I tossed off my towel and slid into the water like an eel, face burning red to the roots of my hair. You weren't allowed to put your head under water, because of microbes, I guess, or splash about. You just sat sedately on submerged seats around the edges of the pool and let the mineral water, which stank like rotten eggs, do all sorts of healing things to your body. After about an hour, you got out with as much dignity as you could, lunging for your towel, and scurried off to the dressing room looking like a par-boiled lobster. My Mum had large, pendulous boobs and she had to keep her arms folded across her chest to restrain them or else they floated to the surface like fleshy buoyancy devices. Naturally, I got the giggles, and bruised ribs where my sister dug her elbow into me. Oh, the humiliation of it all! Little boys were frequently caught drilling holes in the outer fence so they could perve on us. I determined never to set foot in that pool again, so the next time it was announced that we were off for a soak, I went bush. There was a swathe of it behind the holiday house we were renting, so I whiled away the afternoon there curled up with a book, grinning when I heard them all thrashing about and calling for me, until they got fed up and left. As soon as I knew the coast was clear, I crawled out of my hiding place and had a good gorge on the raspberry bushes growing nearby. I had to face the music later when they returned, but it was worth it. Mum told me I was a 'delinquent', which label made me feel further alienated from my family, and kind of exhilaratingly wicked.

Apart from holidays, however fraught on occasions, I loved excursions out to the country during winter to collect sacks of pinecones for the fire from Eyrewell forest. I also smile when I recall the way we chased the whitebait man, hollering and waving the bowls our mothers gave us, when he drove slowly around our neighbourhood streets in his van, bellowing 'white*BAIT!*' out the window. Ten shillings bought one pound of whitebait, which Mum transformed into glistening, golden patties full of little eyes and tiny tails.

Walt Disney and his movies provided me with the fantasy world I longed to escape to. My favourite was *Peter Pan*, and I treasured the comic version I'd bought from the local bookshop, carrying it everywhere with me, until my sister vomited into it while we were watching *The Quiet Man*, and I had to toss the sodden, foul-smelling mess in the Avon River on the way home. I was heartbroken.

All this must convey a sense of an idyllic childhood, apart from the obviously psychotic bits, but these were the norms for life in New Zealand in the fifties/sixties, and beneath the surface it was far from that. I had long since accepted that my mother didn't like me very much, although, as with all my feelings, I never put it into words, since emotional honesty was taboo. I was always aware of my father's prurience, spite, and potential for violence, and my sister's breadknife tongue continued to flay strips off my already lacerated self-esteem with impunity. From the age of thirteen, my mother used me as her sounding board to whine about my father, sharing with me, a child, such salacious details as how he'd belt her one if she declined sex with him, or how he shagged her so often she could hardly hold her head up during the day for fatigue. Such disclosures did nothing to enhance my already wobbly relationship with my father.

Mum was always parasitic on my compassion, but this heightened attribute of mine, ludicrously redundant in my particular family environment, never went any way towards elevating my status on to a par with, or above that, of my hard, self-centred sister.

I've tried to harden up, but it's difficult for me. Older and wiser though, I am now much more circumspect with my compassion.

Then there was our father's wretched hypochondria to deal with. This might not have been so bad had he not had to involve the entire family in his theatrics, which included loud, continuous moaning, a buzz saw-volume forced cough, and such idiocies as eating Vicks Vaporub off a spoon. If anyone, usually my mother, enquired after his wellbeing, he morphed into a snarling, aggressive pitbull; guilt, I suppose. It was like living with a rancorous two-year-old. I hated the tension he generated and his petty minded tyranny that immiserated the whole family. I wanted a father I could look up to, respect, share things with, but he had a hole where his heart should have been and a basically cowardly, shallow disposition. He was small in stature and small in character, a cantankerous, callous, self-absorbed little corporal. I don't say I hated him. But I did feel robbed, and I never felt comfortable around him. I think he wanted to be mothered because his own burned out old mam had been too ground down by hard work and child bearing to give a damn by the time he was born. He'd picked the wrong woman for a substitute mother, though, because Mum was quite cold and hermetic by nature. The only time I ever saw her show genuine affection to any of us was to Michael. He was the apple of her eye. But as he grew older, that love mutated into something mean and possessive, especially when he started having girlfriends. It wasn't ever about our emotional needs; it was about her self-centredness.

I tended to ennoble my mother to the status of resigned martyr as a result of my father's behaviour, and it wasn't until years later that I realised she was just as selfish and narcissistic as he was. Viewed with the detachment of maturity, their relationship finally made sense: they were not ill-matched, as I had always believed growing up; they were kindred spirits.

When I studied poet, James K Baxter, during my Honours year, I came across some lines that could have been written for Mum:

Five children and a fallen womb
A golden crown beyond the tomb

The fifth child was the little baby who never made it.

I finally got my period, at fourteen, much to my sister's delight. At last I had to suffer the same monthly indignities she did. My mother had told us nothing of the facts of life. As small girls, we were often asked to go around to the local shops for her and hand a note to the lady who ran the drapery. The note always said: 'pkt of sp please.' The woman would disappear out the back of the shop and return with a mysterious parcel wrapped in plain brown paper, which we duly delivered home. When curiosity got the better of us and we asked what 'sp' meant, Mum brusquely told us they were 'shoulder pads'. We didn't press it, but we remained puzzled; she didn't sew, and she never wore shoulder pads.

Well, we soon solved the mystery. Travelling home from school one day on the bus, I glanced down and saw to my horror a large patch of blood on my sister's dress. When I drew her attention to it, she was as horrified as I was. We hurried off the bus when we reached our stop, Cheryl desperately trying to hide her bloodied condition from any prying eyes with her school satchel placed strategically over the spreading stain. Convinced she had somehow sustained a terrible wound of fatal proportions, we ran the rest of the way home bawling our eyes out in mutual distress. "Cheryl's dying!" I blurted out as we burst into the house. After the initial shock, Mum set her lips grimly and told us sharply to 'calm down'. She left me sobbing in the kitchen and hustled Cheryl up to her bedroom. When they finally emerged, a transformed Cheryl told me smugly that she had her 'period' and was to all intents and purposes a woman now. I had no clue what she was talking about, especially why being a woman should require such a dramatic rite of passage. At least I now knew what to expect, which was more than my poor sister had.

My sister was given a contraption that resembled a medieval chastity belt with an enormous safety pin suspended back and front, and the mystery of the 'shoulder pads' aka 'sanitary pads' was solved. I found it unfathomable that God would inflict this humiliating monthly trial on women…serious design flaw, oh Creator! The rear safety pin dug cruelly into my coccyx, especially when seated, the blood that gushed forth smelt awful and leaked over the edges of the badly designed pads to stain my panties; the gripping abdominal pains that accompanied the whole wretched process left me pale, sweating and enervated. Sometimes it felt as if my entire viscera were being expelled. When sleeping, you had to put two pads on at once to avoid waking up in the morning to stained pyjamas and sheets, and even this ploy often failed. When I knew my period was due and I was out somewhere, I agonised about the shameful possibility of having a stain appear on the back of my dress or slacks. Biking to school in the summer, wearing my light blue

115

school uniform dress, caused unbearable anxiety also, and I learned to arrange the frock around the saddle so that I was not actually sitting on it. Winter was better because my gym frock was black.

Such is the anguish of the teenaged girl afflicted with 'the curse'. At least one could share the burden with one's close friends as we all commiserated together and supported each other through our trials. And at least Mum provided my sister and me with shop bought sanitary pads. Some of my friends had to use strips of towelling or sheeting that they soaked, washed, dried and re-used. I remember voicing my annoyance over the apparent inequality between male and female physiology to my sister, expressing my disgust that boys got off so lightly in the puberty department. She tossed her head haughtily and disabused me of my ignorance. Boys, she asserted also had their own personal trials: they got 'balls', she informed me triumphantly. I guess I was pretty ignorant, because for days afterwards I carried a mental image of young men expelling something akin to ball bearings from their penises, and wondered how on earth they managed with that discomfort. It went some way to making me feel better, however.

Eventually, I learned to manage my periods fairly well; the pains diminished as I matured, and the monthly bleed settled into a rhythm and volume that no longer caused me too much distress. At the age of thirty-four, after birthing my two babies had left me with a severe prolapse, I was obliged to have a hysterectomy. I was very happy.

Chapter Eight

Another painful adjunct to puberty was acquiring a bra. My nubile elder sister had been happily jiggling around for some time before a prim aunt, who witnessed Cheryl jouncing about while wearing a close-fitting red jersey, scolded my mother for not having her in a bra. Mum was pretty hopeless in the pubescent milestone department. Not only had she not forewarned us of The Curse, but she also seemed oblivious to our growing need for support in the mammary area. Being possessed of very large, pendulous boobs herself, you'd think she would've been more on the ball. Cheryl was duly fitted with a couple of bras from the local draper's, but I would have to wait a while. All my classmates were in bras, but I, alas, was still flat as a pancake. The kids nicknamed me 'eleven'… straight up and down. Eventually, I did swell out in the pectoral area and was suitably restrained. Another developmental hurdle cleared.

Hairy legs were the next source of angst. I'd never had much hair on my legs, but when I became a teenager I noticed with alarm dark hairs appearing on my lower legs. Both my sister and I decided we needed to remove this unsightly growth as quickly as possible. The sensible thing would have been for Mum to buy us a little lady's razor, but she continued to be unsupportive in the grooming and maintenance department. So, we used Dad's razor, sending him off into apoplectic fits of rage when he tried to shave with a blunt blade. Eventually, *he* purchased a razor for us.

Then, of course, acne followed, like the torments of Job. We managed to obtain a product called Valderma, a cream which came in a small tube, and which all the teenaged girls of our acquaintance swore by as a remedy for epidermal embarrassment. This mild anti-bacterial treatment was liberally daubed on our burgeoning pimples every night before we retired to bed. It sort of dried them up, so you were left with a white, flaky patch on your face, which wasn't much of a better look than the pimple.

Makeup. Mum took us both to Woolworths and purchased a tiny Tangee lipstick in a little black case for us to share. It was of a brand considered appropriate for young girls and was very neutral in shade, almost colourless, but which turned to a subtle pink when applied to the lips. We thought we were so grown up, and from there we progressed to eye shadow, mascara, and foundation, with Ponds Cold Cream to remove it all before bed. Curlers were also *de rigueur*, and tiny silver clasps for acquiring kiss curls. We backcombed our hair mercilessly to give it 'body' and froze the ensuing structure of wrecked follicles in place with hair spray. Young men rejected the traditional 'short back and sides' and began to wear their hair longer.

Clothes fashion was also dictated by trend. Girls started to wear slacks more, and tartan was all the rage. Women would not dream of wearing them in the workplace yet, not until the trouser suit fashion emerged. I loved my bobby socks and my apricot half coat, along with a blue velvet dress that had pearl buttons down the front. Black lace mantillas became all the rage for wearing to church. Sneakers were the preferred casual footwear, along with 'flats', while high heeled shoes were a must for going out. Big, flouncy skirts were in, with layers of tulle petticoat underneath. The petticoats even had plastic tubing in the hems, which could be inflated, giving even greater volume. Blouses, shirtwaister frocks, T-shirts, cardigans and boleros were all necessary wardrobe elements, and jeans gradually became popular for both sexes, especially after James Dean popularised them in *Rebel Without a Cause*. The mini skirt was not a good fashion for Kiwi girls, though, as few us have the requisite long, slim legs of our European counterparts. The same caveat applied to hot pants, and, sadly, it was always those with the least suitable limbs that elected to wear these fashions.

Socks and garters had been abandoned once we reached Form 1, and we had suspender belts for holding up our 'nylons'. For school, these had to be of a heavy denier, including lisle, and not too dark, but on weekends we wore more sheer stockings, either seamed or seamless. Getting the seams exactly straight was a challenge. Panty hose eventually made suspender belts redundant.

We were taught dressmaking at school, and all of us made clothes for ourselves: tops, skirts, and dresses. Sewing was never my forte, but I turned out one or two simple garments on Mum's old Singer machine. I was never clothes conscious, and never really interested in them beyond the obvious necessity to be clad in something. It was books that always got me excited, and still do. I can get viscerally aroused just being in a library. My quiet, introspective nature was typically interpreted negatively by my family as 'moodiness'. I was told that I gave 'black looks', that I was 'an angel abroad and a devil at home'. I realise now that these are classic ploys to make the victim of bullying feel that they are the problem, that they have brought the bullying on themselves, but at the time, I just felt more and more worthless and became more and more withdrawn. Over the years, I internalised that there was one standard for me and a different one for everybody else, but I couldn't understand why. This has been consistent throughout my whole life. Animals remained my dearest love.

Then it was on to the next challenge for a teenage girl: the New Zealand male of the species, most of whom adhered to the Kiwi cult of rugged manly mateship, as personified by Barry Crump, and disdained female companionship. This was a time when sex outside marriage was frowned upon, and Catholic girls were expected to retain their virginity for the wedding night. Young men, on the other hand, were expected to lose theirs so that as my sister put it, 'they knew what they were doing' on said wedding night – an age-old double standard which created a considerable quandary for male/female relationships in those times. There were 'good girls' and 'fast girls', and girls who became pregnant while single were said to be 'in trouble'. They had shotgun weddings, or disappeared into maternity homes run by nuns where their babies were subsequently adopted out, as there was no welfare for solo mums in those days. Eventually freely accessible, reliable contraception in the form of the pill simplified matters somewhat.

Anyway, my first experience of boys and dating came when Cheryl's best friend, Frances, asked her to ask me, when I was fourteen, if I'd partner her brother, Lew, to a party. I agreed, and Lew, who had beautiful red hair, picked me up on his bike and carried me, perched on the bar, to the venue, a private home, where the parents lurked inconspicuously but watchfully nearby. A group of about ten partnered teens, we sat around awkwardly, danced a bit, ate some food, and played 'spin the bottle'. A peck on the cheek out in the hallway was as far as the kissing went. Then Lew transported me home by the curfew hour, eleven o'clock. I never saw him again. Apparently, as his date, I was not supposed to dance with other boys. One of his friends subsequently asked me out and I never saw him again, either.

This was the beginning of my total inability to get on the wavelength of the opposite sex. They still remain an area of complete mystery to me. It was only years later that I realised the male of the species has in his DNA a highly sensitive radar for identifying an easy lay. I believe men have an essentially schizoid attitude to women which is summed up in that awful song Rod Stewart wrote for Brit Ekland to commemorate the first time he bedded her… 'Tonight's The Night'. He calls her his 'virgin child' and an 'angel', but then urges her to 'spread her wings and let him come inside' (!). This, to me epitomises the flawed duality of man's approach to woman: he wants her to be both a virgin and a slut simultaneously, and that dichotomy is the root of his misogyny.

By this time I was in the Fourth Form, the age group traditionally associated with rebellious behaviour before settling down for the Fifth Form year and the sobering spectre of School Certificate exams. I wasn't rebellious towards my teachers; my rebellion was deeply spiritual since I was just not at home anywhere. It wasn't that I lacked friends; I just felt dislocated from everything around me and had to maintain a façade of being interested in the same things they were. Glimpses of a beautiful place I yearned for without understanding why tugged at my soul. From the earliest age I was plagued by an unsettling sense of displacement, a feeling that my true home was some place else, and I was heartsick for it. There was no one I felt close enough to with whom I could share these feelings.

The Cold War was in full swing, and the entire free world held its breath over the Cuban missile crisis. There was talk of building fallout shelters, and Nevil Shute's *On the Beach* chilled us all with its depiction of the Apocalypse. The Vietnam War got underway, and President Kennedy's assassination seemed to diminish us all. The arrival of television pulled us into the global village.

In the meantime, my sixteen-year-old sister was now facing the School Certificate ordeal and finding it hard to concentrate since she was *very* interested in the New Zealand male. She failed the exams at the end of the year and subsequently left school with no qualifications, not uncommon in those days. Cheryl was not without ambition, though. When we played with our dolls as children she was fond of saying that she wanted nothing more than to 'be a lady with a baby', while our mother looked on with an expression of doting approval. With Mum's support, she took up an apprenticeship with a city florist, and devoted all her energies to trapping one of those elusive Kiwi lads, who preferred to act like idiots with their male mates rather than enjoy female company. This fervour for the hunt had unfortunate consequences for me, as she frequently insisted I make up one half of a blind date with her current beau's best mate. I lost count of the number of painful liaisons I was dragged out on. One boy refused to talk to me altogether. Another harped on about my inept dancing skills before he finally retired to the back seat of the car we'd arrived in and snored off, leaving me alone and in tears.

I guess, going by the law of averages, I had to get lucky sometime, and I did. Cheryl was going out with a lad called Wayne, and when his cousin, Barry, came to town I was dragged out yet again to provide a date. Barry and I clicked immediately we locked eyes, and after that he regularly came up from Ashburton, where he was a farmer's son, to take me out, or we talked for hours on the phone. At last, I had a soulmate. But my sister soon broke up with Wayne and displaying her customary spite told me I couldn't see Barry anymore. My mother was standing at her elbow, lips drawn thin, daring me to defy this edict, and so I caved as I always did to superior forces. I am certain that a call from Barry was intercepted and he was told not to contact me again.

I still think about Barry. I hope he's happy. I believe my sister resented my newfound happiness and felt compelled to squelch it. Because I had no value in my family, this proved easy. My sister was the first in a long line of bullies that I've had to confront during my life. Later years proved that any bond between us was ephemeral, and now, mature adults, we don't see each other at all. My mother's work is complete.

Disillusioned with matters of the heart, and having internalised the fact that any boyfriend I had in future would always be as disparaged and undervalued as myself, I focused all my efforts on my studies and came out top of my class in my School Certificate year. Following that, I completed two more years of secondary education before leaving to go to University and study for an Arts degree. I got a holiday job that year in a dreadful Dickensian sweatshop in St Asaph Street, the Christchurch Hospital Laundry, and began to save money for the next few destitute years of being a student. I continued to live at home because I was too poor to leave.

When I entered the hallowed halls of Canterbury University, I was seventeen, and totally without any self esteem, confidence, or any sense of belonging in time and place. I was riddled with insecurities and had no idea who I was, any self-awareness subsumed in my urgency to please others, to make them like me, believing that I was the one at fault for my lack of value to those who were supposed to love me. I was all fragments, bits and pieces, because I had never been enabled to develop as a whole person, to be who I truly am and to let others know that, too.

Chapter Nine

Canterbury University, built in 1877, was a striking greystone gothic-style complex not far from the banks of the Avon River and opposite the Christchurch Botanical Gardens, a place I loved. Apart from the lecture theatres and Great Hall, there was a beautiful clock tower, lovely quads and porticos, a splendid library, and a student union building that housed a café selling cheap food. You could get a pie, peas, and mashed potatoes for 30c. I loved it all, especially the library. In my first year, I studied English, French, and History, with a view to obtaining a BA degree, majoring in English.

My parents were indifferent to my decision to go on to higher learning. They seemed to believe I would leave school and get a job like my sister, who was already engaged to be married to a complete dropkick of a bloke. Of course, one could not give expression to this opinion, as he was my sister's boyfriend and therefore immune from all criticism. It didn't last, and she was soon back on the prowl. In the 60's, a young man's hope of regular sex still largely meant marriage, so she had that on her side. A considerable area of our bedroom was now taken up by one of those awful pieces of furniture called 'a glory box', which clucky young women crammed full of trousseau and other bits and pieces deemed necessary for the matrimonial condition. I shuddered every time I looked at it. Having the example of our parents' far from happy marriage in front of her, I had to question why she was so keen to enter the state herself.

The three years I spent at university were just a continuation of my, by now entrenched, sense of loneliness and isolation. I made a couple of new friends, and enjoyed some lectures more than others, but, overall, I found the courses uninspiring and dry. I bluffed my way through my degree by drawing on my ability to write very good prose about nothing; in short, I waffled convincingly. I didn't read a single one of the prescribed texts, just pertinent reviews and summaries which I skillfully paraphrased. The last two years of my high school education in English had been spent under the auspices of a dear old, over-the-hill Irish nun called Sister Croinaofa (Irish Gaelic for 'Sacred Heart'), and while she was sweet and entertaining – I especially loved her stories about a childhood friend she'd had with the unlikely name of Foncey Smiley – she didn't teach us a jot, and I had no idea how to critique literature by its essential elements of theme, character, plot, and setting. In retrospect, I should have been doing a creative writing course, the like of which are now available, but didn't exist back then. I was never part of the 'in crowd', kids from wealthy Christchurch families who belonged to cliques like the Ski Club, and men remained an enigma for me – the New Zealand species, anyway. During my three years at Canterbury, I only had one serious, semi-long distance, relationship with a young Australian man I met in during a weekend in Queenstown chaperoning my sister. I thought for a while that he was my soulmate, but our relationship eventually foundered over his deteriorating grip on reality and insistence on living like some kind of social refugee. I was, and still am, a hopeless romantic.

I attended the requisite student parties, of course, but they were so boring and conformed to such a mind-numbingly predictable pattern of futility, that I gave up. The boys all focused on getting drunk – to stress the point, engineering students wore their beer mugs on chains around their necks – singing lewd songs, and getting laid, while the simpering girls stood around watching their antics, like projectile vomiting. By midnight, as if Cinderella's fairy godmother had waved her wand, everyone suddenly quit the whole farce and went home.

In the varsity holidays, I worked to earn money, doing a variety of jobs that involved rote or mindless manual labour: sorter in the hospital laundry, flour and sugar bagger, petrol pump attendant, car detailer, theatre usher, and fruit picker. Thus, I had a break from the halls of academia and learned how the working class suffered. The hospital laundry employees were predominantly women, and the working conditions were appalling. In the summer months, the temperature inside the place was in the 90sF° and I sweated off pounds in weight. Health and safety were non-existent concepts, and there were some awful accidents with the heavy ironing presses. The girls at those presses stood on their feet all day for what was often an eleven-hour shift, no evening meal provided. One young woman was heavily pregnant, with badly swollen legs, but she was shown no special sympathy. They just provided her with a basin of cold water to stand in.

Although I was an impoverished student, I bought my mother presents that I hoped would win me her affection: a pigskin handbag she coveted, an ikebana vase she'd enthused over. I should have saved my money. When the scapegoat does something perceived as being inconsistent with their assigned character, for example something generously positive that might indicate a noble rather than a debased nature, the response is going to be muted, if not dismissive.

I always had to be careful what I did, or what I said, and I never learned. I remember once we were at the table eating breakfast, and I was buttering a piece of toast. The mood was relatively benign, so I gaily quipped, "Butter your edges well," a favourite mantra of my father's, who considered toast buttering something of an art. The next moment, he was in my face snarling invective at me for 'mocking him'. The hurt and bewilderment were awful, and I fled to my room.

It was during this time that my beloved little dog, Heidi, died suddenly. I'd patted her goodbye as I did every morning before leaving for work, and by the time I arrived home she was dead and buried. While I was still dealing with her loss, my father carried out one of his typical assassinations on my only remaining pet, my sweetheart of a cat, Louis. I found Louis when I went to visit a friend one day in my school holidays. He was desperately hungry, a bedraggled stray, and had been hanging around my friend's house for a while, begging for food. My friend's mother, an otherwise nice person, refused to feed him and said she would 'take him for a ride in the country'. I am always staggered when otherwise good people display this kind of shocking lack of compassion to an animal in need. I have witnessed it many times. When I left that afternoon, I stuffed the frail Louis into the pannier bag attached to the back of my bike and carried him home, bracing myself, as I pedalled, to face the music. To my surprise, I was permitted to keep him. Big, fluffy back and white boy, he had a gorgeous nature, affectionate, gentle and very laid back. He never left my side and slept with me every night. As one who felt perennially unloved, I appreciated his devotion and adored him in turn. One day, after about two years, I noticed he had a bit of diarrhoea, and was visiting the garden more than was usual for him. I believe now that my father had poisoned him because he later did the same to my mother's Maltese terrier, and the next day when I got up Louis had disappeared. His sin, apart from being precious to me, had been toileting, like any normal cat, in my father's pristine garden. My mother watched me hunting high and low for him and, although she almost certainly knew what my father had done, she said nothing. A long time later, my father told my sister he'd abducted Louis and finished him off, news she gleefully imparted to me. I was utterly heartbroken and still mourn my beloved old cat all these years later. Of course, my sister provided the definitive verdict the day he disappeared and I was desperately searching for him: "It's just an old cat."

While I worked at the hospital laundry, I had one of several experiences in my life when someone I had never met before, who was neither acquainted with me nor me with them, apparently hated me on sight. This person was the man who arrived every Thursday morning with our pay packets. He took up station behind a small table brought on to the workshop floor for the purpose, and senior staff ushered us up in batches to sign for and collect our pay. Once collected, the wise not only stuffed their hard-earned cash inside their underwear, but fastened it there with large safety pins, as women were ruthlessly robbed every week. Alice, my supervisor, had explained this necessity to me on my first day of work, and I always followed her advice to the letter.

The pay clerk was a tall, pleasant-looking man, probably in his thirties, with thick, tightly-clipped, black hair, wearing a business suit. He smiled and joked with the girls and women as the queue edged towards him, being especially convivial with the old hands. The very first time I approached him, he asked me, unsmilingly, for the first letter of my surname and I said 'A'. When he flipped the ledger over to the A's page, there was, however, no sign of my name in that list. In an attempt to be helpful, I explained that I was casual staff, a university student, so my name could be in a separate, temporary group. There were a few students employed there.

Instantly, as if some deep-seated grievance had been prodded into life, his demeanour changed from friendly to overtly hostile. Flipping over pages, my name was eventually found and the ledger almost hurled at me for my signature. Once I'd signed, my pay was hurled in my direction with similar animus. I slunk away bewildered.

Every week thereafter, we played out this unpleasant ritual: me, heart thumping, unable to locate my name, him snatching the book back after he felt I'd endured sufficient humiliation, then hurling it back at me along with the little brown envelope containing my pay. All the while, he fairly quivered with barely suppressed hatred, dark eyes burning with contempt, leaving me with the same question each time: Why? What had I done to him? Even though I wanted my pay, I dreaded its collection every Thursday.

I had a similar experience to that one when I was about twelve. A school friend had asked me to accompany her for an afternoon's rowing on the Avon River, a popular pastime in Christchurch. It was a lovely summer's day, so I agreed, and we caught the bus to town before making our way to the Antigua Street boatsheds. I was quite a pretty kid, and on that day, quite incidentally, I was wearing a short-sleeved cotton dress decorated with little anchors and other nautical items, my dark hair fastened back in a ponytail. The man in charge of hiring out the boats took one look at me and began to seethe with hatred. After issuing instructions to my friend, as we boarded our canoe, in a cheerful and helpful manner, he then turned into a nasty, snarling antithesis as he addressed me, belittling my efforts to push off and start paddling, his ugly reprimands following us as we headed off upstream, me feeling desperate to escape his irrational wrath and the pitying looks from the other people waiting to hire boats. The 'bystanders' is the correct term, I believe. My 'friend' proved to be a bystander also.

The afternoon was ruined, as all I could think of was having to face the horrible man again. Eventually, time up, we had to return, and my heart sank when we rounded the last bend to see him standing at the edge of the boathouse decking, peering up the river as if he were waiting just for us. He was, and as soon as we hove into view, he began his rant. I was 'you in the back', and he gradually became more and more hysterical as he shouted out the errors I was apparently making with my every manoeuvre to ease the canoe out of the current and alongside the decking for retrieval purposes. In the end, I just shipped my paddle, which provoked a particularly virulent outburst of rage, and left my friend to it, since she could do no wrong, it seemed. Throughout my tormentor's harangue, members of the public watched me being abused without comment. I was shaking so hard, I could barely get out of the canoe, and, in my haste, left my little change purse on the seat, provoking one final, sarcastic scream of reprimand.

I have no idea why the pay clerk or the boatman hated me on sight, but I have pondered it often. Did the pay clerk resent my university status, or imagine I was bragging about it? Did my nautically inspired dress inflame the boatman? I really have no idea, but my family had trained me well, and I had no comeback against such irrational hatred. Clearly, I have the unmistakeable mark of the scapegoat, like some kind of brand of Cain, but how one is selected for this role, the human dynamics behind the identification, the unspoken invitation to project one's self-loathing on to another person, remains a mystery to me.

I once had the temerity to ask my parents what it meant to be the 'black sheep' of a family. The scathing mockery was swift in response. Did I feel hard done by? Perhaps if I were nicer-more-likeable-tried harder etc I'd be less of an outsider.

It was almost as if I had to self-flagellate to confirm the futility of ever improving my status within my family.

Meanwhile, the steady erosion of my self-esteem continued unabated:

"Your eye makeup makes your eyes look smaller."

"Your hair makes you look like Yoko Ono."

"You and your friend remind me of the two girls who murdered the mother up on the hills."

"You had a date once, didn't you?" (mocking laughter)

"You're childish and over-emotional."

"Did he ask you out? You poor thing."

And so on. I was, I concluded, possessed of some fatal flaw, like the hamartia of a Shakespearean character, that singled me out for victimisation and precluded me from respect as a fellow human being.

In my second year of tertiary study, my family was involved in an event of major proportions: my sister's wedding. She was only twenty, but she had bagged her man after a few false starts, the date for the nuptials was set, April 23rd 1966, and the entire household was thrown into pre-marital upheaval. The groom, a young man of German descent, was a professional student who lived off his wealthy parents and, at the age of twenty-five, had no career prospects whatsoever. But he was my sister's choice, and therefore immune from all speculation re his suitability as husband material. He converted to Catholicism, as marriage between a Catholic and a Protestant was verboten in those days, and plans proceeded for a full church service followed by a lavish reception at the Brevet Club, a trendy venue at the time. I was to be one of two bridesmaids, along with my sister's best friend. We wore dresses of dark green shantung silk and white flowers in our hair, while my sister naturally chose a princess crown to top off her virginal white attire and veil. It was after all, a right royal occasion.

There is a photo taken on that wedding day of my sister and me, our mother, our younger brothers, and two of our aunts standing on the sundeck at the back of the house as festivities were winding down. (The men were all segregated in the garage guzzling from a large keg of beer). My sister looks happy, my mother looks happy; everyone looks happy, in fact. I, on the other hand, look plaintively sad. That's because I know in my heart that my lowly status rules out the possibility of my ever enjoying an equivalent celebration. On cue, some years later, when I became engaged, my mother took me aside and told me not to expect a wedding like my sister's. She should have known I never had. My father had sent her to do his hatchet job. I did not protest. It was the way things were, and I just accepted it as befitting for one of no value, like myself. I also overheard her whinging to my sister that she would have to 'look after' the only guests we had invited, long term friends of Phil, outside of a few family members. The guests numbered two and were staying in a motel. My mother was the most inhospitable person I have ever encountered.

Anyway, at last I had the bedroom to myself...but not for long.

After nine years of socialising and the odd bit of study, my brother-in-law had gained his BA, and following their honeymoon, he and my sister went to live in Auckland, where his parents also resided, making it easier for him to pick up the cheques his father regularly wrote out for him. My mother was heartbroken, but I was delighted to a) have my own room at last and b) to be free of the nasty put downs and ridicule regularly meted out by my sister. I could breathe a lot easier, even though living with my cranky father still grated on my nerves.

The next event of any excitement was the news that my sister was pregnant, the baby expected in March 1967. (Good Catholic girl… the wedding date cleared by three months.) My mother grew even sadder about being so far from this milestone event: the birth of her first grandchild. I had a deep sense of foreboding. My instincts did not fail me. The first trial came when my sister insisted my mother come up to Auckland for the expected grandchild's birth. The sensible thing would have been to wait until the baby was born, and then for Mum to go up, using her experience to assist with the adjustment to the new motherhood phase. But no. My sister pointlessly wanted her right then, weeks before the baby was due. So, of course, my mother went, leaving me to look after the home and its occupants for over a month and somehow fit in my lectures and university commitments at the same time. My father made things intolerable by demanding that I cook the most outrageously complicated meals, sophisticated dishes that we never normally had, and being a novice cook I found very challenging. I lost pounds in weight and came close to a breakdown, which was averted when my father, fed up with my disappointing culinary achievements, phoned my mother and ordered her home, ironically just after their grandson had finally made his appearance, the first of four children born to my sister and her husband, all boys. I was so happy that I prepared a special lunch for her. During the flight to Christchurch, she had been a little airsick and was not happy with the matter-of-fact care doled by the stewardesses, so she staggered off the plane, ignored me, griped all the way home, stalked past my beautifully laid-out luncheon and put herself to bed. She didn't even thank me for holding the fort for over a month, or notice the weight I'd lost.

After that shaky start to the year, things settled down a bit and I focused on getting good grades for my BA finals, as I had it in the back of my mind to do a Master's. The news from

Auckland continued to be despondent: my sister's husband still had no job, and her mother-in-law, she insisted, wanted to kidnap the baby. Two spoilt offspring in tandem makes a bad combination when confronted with the harsh realities of life.

One night, just as I was going to bed, my mother took a phone call from my sister. They chatted for quite a while, and when the call finished my mother came into my room, wearing her passion-killer flannel nightie, and stood in the doorway with a strange look on her face. I tensed. With an air of defiance, Mum informed me that Cheryl was coming back to Christchurch and bringing the baby with her. She hated Auckland and her mother-in-law. No, she was not breaking up with her husband. He'd be down later. Then she told me the really bad news. I had to vacate my room for Cheryl and the child and go elsewhere. Shocked and bewildered, a penurious student, I asked where I was meant to go. I needed a quiet place to study, after all. She shrugged and said she didn't know. Then she went out, closing the door behind her. Of all the hurts I endured, that one has stayed with me the longest and cut the deepest.

For the next three months, I slept on the narrow, uncomfortable couch in our living room. Nobody cared if I was tired or if I needed to go to bed. I had to wait until the last person was finished watching TV before I could crawl into my sleeping bag. I had no privacy. If I wanted to study, I had to traipse back to the university library at night after dinner. Retrieving clothes or personal belongings from my room meant stepping over milk puddles on the polished wooden floor, as my sister grappled with the messy business of breast feeding. My mother spent all her time doting on her eldest daughter, who did not even apologise for the inconvenience I suffered, and her grandchild. I was invisible, utterly worthless, undeserving of any consideration. Well trained in my role by now, I did not protest. Not once.

I slept on that hard old couch from September to December, right through my BA finals. I passed everything and gained my degree at age twenty. It could be time, I thought, to leave a home where I was clearly surplus to requirements and make my own way in the world. I'd taken out a teaching studentship in my last year of university so that I had some steady income, and now I had to complete my one-year post-graduate training at Teachers' College. It seemed I was destined for the teaching profession, at least for the one year that I owed the government, anyway. The country was desperately short of teachers at the time, especially high school teachers, and there were tons of jobs. I knew I was just drifting into the profession, but I had no one to take an interest in me or offer me any guidance, no one with whom I could discuss my career options. I was a non-person.

My sister and her husband had reunited and settled in Christchurch, much to my mother's delight. I had my bedroom back at last. Many years later, when my sister was lecturing me on how she had left home early, as if this were somehow a personal achievement, I reminded her that she had come back almost immediately, leaving me stateless for several months. She was instantly defensive, offering no apology and displaying not a jot of empathy for the situation she'd put me in. She seemed to be totally unaware of any disruption she had caused to my life and annoyed that I should feel aggrieved about it. Why would she? I had no value. Now that she was back in the bosom of her family, it was taken for granted that I would babysit on demand, often minding her growing family for whole weekends while she and her husband had a 'break', to cook pots of chicken soup for her when she was poorly, and generally be on hand to provide support, all with Mum's direct connivance. Oh yes, I knew my place.

ERIN ELDRIDGE

Chapter Ten

My graduation played out true to form. I had some invitation slips for family and friends, so my sister and parents agreed, with a marked lack of enthusiasm, to attend. My sister informed me that the capping ceremony was 'nothing special', just in case I got any ideas above my station. She knew this, she added, having witnessed her husband's graduation previously. "You just go up in a bunch," she snapped, twitching one nostril sideways in her unattractive, rabbity quirk, which signalled no argument.

After the ceremony, I invited everyone to come for a drink to celebrate. My father looked at his watch and said he had to get back to work. My mother and sister left with him. Alone, I wandered into town and bought some cooked chickens from a favourite deli, along with two bottles of Crackling Rosé wine. Once home, (my father had spent the afternoon reading in bed) I prepared my celebration meal to share with them all on my own. There was no present to mark the occasion. No photos. Two years later, when I graduated with my Masters, that achievement was ignored in similar fashion.

Five years later, when I was working in Africa, my parents sent me photos of my brother Michael's graduation. My parents, positioned on either side of him, beamed proudly at the camera, and the accompanying letter described the celebration dinner out at a top restaurant. He'd been gifted a watch to mark the occasion. I stared at the photo for a long time. How did they imagine this contrast with my own graduation would make me feel? Were they even aware of how they treated me that day? Did they even recall it? How I felt, was of no consequence, apparently.

A friend of a few years had asked me to go flatting with her and I accepted, feeling the time was right and wanting to be free from the wearying tensions at home. When I told my mother, she was furious, pointing out that I had a perfectly good home and no need she could see to leave it. Then she withdrew behind a barrier of weepy, wounded, self-righteous indignation that made me feel wracked with guilt. I knew why she wanted me to stay, and it had nothing to do with what I wanted, what might be good for me, or make me happy. She didn't want to lose her sounding board for her continuous whining about my father. When she wasn't whining about him, for some inexplicable reason she martyred herself to make this utterly shallow, selfish, callous man as comfortable as she could, ensuring that he was pampered, indulged, and shielded from anything that might provoke his cantankerous, infantile disposition. I have encountered a few of these child/adults in the course of my life, and for some unfathomable reason they are always indulged with a tolerance and patience, a kindness not shown to the rest of us. Human nature is indeed a mystery.

One night, when my father was having one of his hypochondriacal tantrums, screeching and moaning in the bedroom, he flung Mum across the room in front of us when she went in to see what was wrong. I snapped, and although I was shaking I read him his pedigree. You could have heard a pin drop. He didn't speak to me for three weeks, which was great, but it fixed him, and the idiotic theatrics abruptly stopped. The irony was, of course, that he enjoyed excellent health, for which he was not in the least bit grateful. To my dismay, my sister and Mum turned on me for 'upsetting your father'. I'd broken the cardinal rule of 'keeping the peace', of pretending everything was just fine and dandy. I felt unable to stomach the hypocrisy any longer and left to take my chances with my peers.

The flat in question was a little old cottage in Hastings Street, Sydenham, an old and charming area of the city, where lots of streets were named after English poets. If it had just been me and my friend flatting, I believe we would have been all right, but to cover the rent for such a dwelling, we had to take in two additional flatmates, both strangers, and things did not go well following this altered dynamic. I should have tried harder and I know I let my friend down, but by the time a terribly stormy Easter came, with the media full of the tragic sinking of the inter-islander ferry, *Wahine,* I called it quits and went home, the lesson that I did not fare well living with other people well internalised. My mother was delighted. I tried so hard to please her. I cooked, cleaned, sewed, painted, gardened. But when the chips were down, I always came in second best.

Teachers' College was odd, to say the least. Our tutor had serious marital issues with his new wife and was often away, leaving us to our own devices. The other graduates in my group were easy enough to get along with, and so I coasted through the year, the highlights of which were the teaching placements we were sent on. My first section, as the hands-on experiences in actual schools were called, was at Cottesmore, a relatively new snobby Catholic college for girls in Riccarton (The girls wore boaters). The four weeks I spent there were uneventful and I mostly observed other teachers in their classrooms, trying hard to look keen and taking copious notes.

My second placement was at Westland High School in Hokitika, just after the Inangahua earthquake had devastated the region, leaving all the chimneys down. I stayed with a kindly, hospitable old woman of German descent, Mrs Mehrtens, who had raised eight kids and was a great cook. She must have missed the clamour of a large family because, with all her kids gone from the nest, she filled her home with boarders, both temporary, like myself, or long term. Her happiness the day her chimney was repaired was unbounded, and that night we had a roaring fire, Mrs Mehrtens parked solidly in front of it, skirts pulled up, legs spread, repeating in reverent tones, "A fire's a living thing. It's a living thing." I nodded dreamily as I scraped up the last remnants of apple crumble and fresh cream from my dessert bowl. During the night, the sea, only a row of houses away, would begin roaring, signalling the arrival of a series of aftershocks, and my little camp stretcher bed in the front room would sway alarmingly back and forth until they stopped. This was my first experience of the West Coast and the beginning of a life-long love affair, despite the tremors.

For my final section, I begged to be allowed to go to the Coast again, and Mr Chalmers, my tutor, indulged me. This time I went up north, to the beautiful area of Karamea, where I was billeted with a sole-charge teacher, Athol, his wife, Sandy, and their little girl. I have a fond memory of arriving at Westport railway station in the early hours of the morning and being led to an armchair in front of a glowing coal fire in the station master's office, where he fetched me a cup of hot tea to drink while I waited for daylight and the bus to take me on to my destination. I was the only traveller on the bus and the elderly driver insisted I sit up front and chat with him. At one point, he stopped and bought me an ice cream. Coasters...salt of the earth. The kindness of strangers always throws into stark relief the unkindness of those whom you trust to have your best interests at heart.

There were only twenty-odd students in the entire high school, which was part of a 'district school' that comprised primary and secondary on one site. About three local families seemed to supply most of the kids, who were shy and biddable. The principal was a great guy and the atmosphere decidedly relaxed. On days when word flew around the tiny settlement that the whitebait were on the run, school closed and we all dashed off across the paddocks to the river with our nets. The coastal scenery was breathtakingly beautiful and unspoiled, the locals friendly and welcoming, the teaching undemanding. Saturday nights in the local pub were the highlight of the week, and the local cop ignored the closing hours. He was there drinking with us. I did not want to leave.

At the end of the year, I graduated with my teaching diploma, but I did not want to go teaching. Not yet, anyway. I knew I was just drifting into it without harbouring any real enthusiasm for the profession. While everyone else in my group was madly seeking for jobs, I applied to Victoria University in Wellington to study for my Master of Arts degree, choosing the Honours course. Their English department had a very good reputation, and I was also desperate to get away from home. I was accepted, and a friend I'd made at college who wanted to do the same course asked me if I was interested in sharing digs with her. I was, and we ended up sharing a flat on the eleventh floor of a large apartment building on Clifton Terrace, a cable car ride from the university. A friend of hers who was starting her first teaching job in the city made up the third member of our ménage. By now, I was twenty-one, and Mum seemed to accept, albeit reluctantly, that from now on I would be coming and going at best, but not living long-term at home anymore.

The year at Victoria was one of the best of my life. While I did not make any lifelong friends, the other students on the course, male and female, were a good bunch and the staff were brilliant, treating us like equals and in amongst all the hard work throwing some legendary parties for us where we danced our asses off to the music from 'Hair'. Neil Armstrong walked on the moon and we too felt we could shoot for the stars.

Merriment and the heady aspirations of youth aside, there was a lot of hard work and study to get through. One of my tutors, Professor Joan Stevens, pulled me up early on over my bad old habit of 'proficient waffle' – she labelled it 'gabbledygook' – and showed me how to properly analyse literature. After my first A grade my confidence soared. I passed all my final papers well and was now officially Erin Anderson, MA (Hons). Time to find a job. I had to teach for at least one year under the terms of my studentship.

Chapter Eleven

I worked all over the summer, detailing cars for the showroom of a prominent vehicle dealer in Christchurch, as well as working nights as a theatre usher. The Masters year had left me with some considerable debt to pay off. I also obtained my driver's licence at this time, to increase my independence. I applied for jobs in Christchurch, but had no luck. At one interview, the pompous ass of a headmaster asked me which character in *Hamlet* I most pitied. Outraged, I nevertheless replied politely that I had the degree; now I needed a job. He looked most affronted, and the rejection slip arrived a few days later. This was my first intimation that highly qualified women in the teaching profession were not exactly greeted with enthusiasm, especially if they were better qualified than their overlords.

Eventually, I accepted a position at Gore High School in Southland. I didn't even know where the place was and had to look it up on a map. I placed an advertisement in the local paper and got one reply from a man who assured me that he had a nice little place to rent, 'fully furnished'. I had no vehicle. I'd asked my father if he could lend me some money to get one, as I was going to be salaried and would pay him off quickly. I had my eye on a neat little Mini Cooper pickup with leather racing seats, which was for sale at my workplace for a mere $1800. My father declined. Some time later he helped my brother get his first car when he took up his first teaching job, also in Southland. I happened to be at home when he turned up for one school holiday break, driving said car. My father must have suffered pangs of conscience, as he sidled up to me in the kitchen one morning and muttered defensively, "I didn't have any spare money when you needed a car." We both knew that wasn't true. I didn't even react, just kept on with whatever I was doing, and he stalked off muttering. Sons and daughters were poles apart when the favours were being dispensed. He delivered me to the railway station to catch the night train, and I left Christchurch for the great unknown with a suitcase and $12 in my pocket.

My prospective landlord met me at the station in Gore as pre-arranged, and drove me, groggy from lack of sleep, to my flat. When he unlocked the front door, I was taken aback to see that the hallway floor was hidden under a carpet of dead leaves.

"The kids play in here," he explained, waving a hand airily. "You can borrow our spare vacuum cleaner."

As I tried to make sense of this bizarre introduction to my new abode, he conducted me on a quick tour. On the right, inside the door, there was a front room cum lounge with a solitary red armchair and a fireplace. Just beyond the lounge, on the same side of the house, was a large bedroom with a lonely single bed and mattress, a narrow wardrobe, and featuring an old tiled fireplace that had been blocked off. Beyond the bedroom, turning right through a telephone alcove, was a tiny kitchen with a stove, fridge, table, and three chairs. At the very end of the hallway, on the other side of the kitchen, there was a combined shower room, laundry, and toilet with a washbasin, mirror, and an ancient, rusting agitator washing machine. There was no bedding, cutlery, crockery, pots and pans, kettle or other chattels. Clearly, I had misinterpreted 'fully furnished'.

The house, on a corner section, was an antiquated villa, which had been converted to two flats, and mine comprised half of the front right hand side of the house. Beyond the steps to the entrance grew thickly overgrown and unfenced lawn with an odd little statue of a white plaster dolphin rearing out of the lush grass near a drunkenly leaning letterbox.

Mr Stein, who was Dutch, beamed happily as he deposited my bulging suitcase in the bedroom and handed me the key. "There you are now. Come over and have dinner with us tonight." He pointed. "I'm just across the road, number forty-two. Come at six." He turned to go, then stopped, extending a hand. "I'll be needing a week's rent in advance, eleven dollars."

With heart sinking, I handed over the money, and he left me to it. I had only one dollar and some loose coins to survive on until payday, whenever that might be. I had not yet even filled out the requisite forms for getting on to the payroll. Feeling rather lost and alone, I crunched my way back through the dead leaves to the bedroom to begin unpacking.

Having sorted my meagre belongings, I tidied the hallway leaves into something resembling a tidy pile, locked up, and headed off towards the high school, which was about half a mile away, and which opened for the beginning of the new school year the following day. I didn't know if anyone would be in attendance, but I felt I should put in an appearance, just in case, to let someone know I had arrived.

As it happened, there were quite a few staff on site, mainly management, preparing for the coming school year. I met the Principal (he was called 'The Rector'), a fairly gruff sort of chap, and my head of department for English, a Mr Meiklejohn, who was blasé and abrupt, barely welcoming. He claimed no one had advised him I was coming, and he was very annoyed about it. With some introductions made and the time I should pitch up to begin work the following day established, I wandered off to town to see what I could find to eat for a dollar. I hadn't eaten since my last dinner at home.

The township was spread out along both sides of a very wide main street running through the middle of town, which had a prosperous air about it, as farming towns in the 70s did everywhere in New Zealand. The cars parked outside the shops and businesses, I noted, comprised luxury vehicles in generous measure: Jensen Healeys, Jaguars, Mercedes, Daimlers, MGs. This was a service town for local wealthy farmers, and it had the feel of comfortable, complacent affluence. About eight miles away, was the comparatively proletariat freezing works town of Mataura, a stark contrast to Gore.

I strolled about for a bit, getting the lay of the land, noting the whereabouts of places like the bank, bought a bag of apricots from a Four Square store down a side street, and wandered off home, feeling miserable and alone. Once home inside my gloomy flat, I sat in the red chair, ate one apricot, and waited for six o'clock to come around.

Mr Stein had a large brood of kids and a resigned looking wife. Dinner was fish and it was very nice, although I was so hungry I would have devoured anything that looked remotely like food. After dinner, I lingered a while, watching some TV, and then Mr Stein escorted me 'home', carrying the promised vacuum cleaner, which looked antediluvian. It blew up, belching evil, black fumes, the first time I tried to use it.

That first week of my teaching career was one of the most difficult of my life. I lived on an apricot a day and could feel the weight falling off me. A lot of the time I was light-headed and spacey. I was allocated a classroom and met the levels I was going to be teaching. Apart from one brattish Fourth Form group they seemed okay. The school had a real cross-section of Southland society on its roll: the town dwellers' kids, the offspring of local well-to-do farmers, and the knuckle draggers from Mataura. The latter made up most of the low stream classes and some of them were truly terrifying, like extras from *Deliverance*. My HOD was markedly absent as I tried to settle in, and I deduced, correctly as it turned out, that I could not expect much support from that pompous old bachelor who did little to conceal his misogyny. At night, I slept on a bare mattress in my clothes and wept with loneliness and hunger.

By the end of the week, I had made a resolution to hire a car and drive up to Christchurch to pick up the things I needed to make life more bearable, and phoned my parents to let them know. My mother promptly had the vapours over the dangers inherent in this mission and took to her bed, as she always did in a perceived crisis. It was, after all, all about her. My sister then called me and told me, in her best imperious tone, that I was not to undertake the drive as I had upset my mother. At least I was spared the unpleasant sight of the accompanying nostril twitch. I pointed out that nobody had been upset about letting me leave home with no money and only a few items of clothing, or that I was living like a refugee and badly needed to collect some furnishings, but she remained intransigent. Giving her my word I would not do the drive, I hung up, and then continued with my arrangements.

First, I phoned a local car-hire firm and booked a vehicle. Then, I approached the less-than-friendly Rector, Douglas Olsen, and asked for an advance on my salary. This was not the era of credit cards, and I had no collateral with which to secure a loan, so I was at his mercy. He was a strange, remote individual who had not endeared himself to the locals by addressing the kids as 'peasants' and 'hayseeds' at his first assembly. He was not hands on, spurned the very idea of regular staff meetings, and holed up in his office, singing opera arias at the top of his voice. This was my first intimation, due to be consolidated with further experience, that most school bureaucrats are promoted beyond their level of competence, and that the more grandiose the title of the position, the more inversely proportionate the skills of the incumbent. This sad reality was frequently enabled by the pernicious practice of giving non-comps glowing references to get rid of them. Once ensconced in their new position, they wreaked havoc, often bringing whole schools down. When a fish rots, it starts at the head. I was to witness a horrifying example years later while teaching in Gisborne. Another story.

Anyway, after droning on about how he frowned upon such practices as doling out advances between official pay dates, he finally gave me some money from the school's petty cash, and I raced off as soon as the final bell sounded to pick up my rental, a nice little Mini. Despite the company's misgivings over the fact that I'd only had my driver's licence for two weeks, my heartfelt pleading saw the paperwork speedily completed, and off I went, totally in the wrong direction, headed further south. I soon realised my mistake, however, did a u-turn and belted back the way I'd come before heading to Dunedin. The distance I had to cover would take me about nine hours, especially since the car had a governor on its speed.

I drove and drove, and soon darkness fell. I had filled up with petrol in Palmerston, but by the time I reached Ashburton, just one hour from Christchurch, I ran out of petrol and glided on to the berm by the highway cursing myself for being such an idiot. It was 1a.m. There were no twenty-four hour petrol stations in those days so I should have packed a jerry can and funnel. As I sat in the little car by the side of the road, feeling frustrated and wretched, I saw some approaching headlights and stepped out to wave whoever it was down, not even thinking about putting myself in danger. The pick-up's occupant turned out to be a young local farmer and, after I explained my predicament, he told me to sit tight and raced off to pick up a jerry can of petrol from his farm. I wondered if he really would return, but he was true to his word, and after filling my tank for me he refused to take any payment. A true guardian angel. I have encountered many such angels during the course of my life. Elated and grateful, I sped on towards Christchurch, arriving exhausted but proud of myself around one in the morning.

After the initial blast of disapproval from my parents, they expressed reluctant admiration for my courage, and set about loading me up with whatever spare household goods they had, which were a lot, since Mum had a passion for collecting kitchenware and other domestic trivia. I ate everything in sight, slept for hours on the Saturday night, and headed off early Sunday morning back to Gore, the little car loaded to the gunnels and a box of food tucked away as well.

The journey was uneventful, and I pulled into the flat's 'driveway' (some ruts in the grass to one side of the house) not long after dark, unloaded my stuff, made my bed, and slept soundly until my alarm went off Monday morning. While I'd been away, Mr Stein had added a red couch to complement the red armchair in my lounge, and once I'd sorted away all my new domestic acquisitions, the place was beginning to look like a home of sorts. Stein later told me that he'd thought I'd done a runner when I disappeared over the weekend. I was delighted to see that the leaves had been removed from the hallway, too, improving the general appearance of the flat. Stein wouldn't get the cleaner fixed, though. I had to do that myself, and, as I'd suspected, it needed a new motor. After its transplant, it performed well.

The next morning, freshly showered, as I boiled my kettle and made and ate breakfast, my morale soared, and once I'd delivered the trusty Mini safely back to the relieved hire firm I headed off to school with a spring in my step, and my clothes fitting loosely from all the weight I'd lost. When lessons finished that day, I dropped off a list of basic grocery items at the local Four Square and the friendly owner delivered them to me in a cardboard box about an hour later. I stocked up my little kitchen cupboards with all the necessities of life, including tomato sauce and Vegemite. That night I had steak, egg, and chips for dinner. Bliss.

Gore High School had a big roll and a large complement of staff to match. As a newcomer, and shy by nature, I kept to myself, but I did start to get to know people and make some friends. There was a highly intelligent young woman, Myrlwynn, a Mataura local and old girl of the school, with whom I struck up an immediate rapport, an older, motherly woman, Kay Domigan, and a father and son teaching duo, Jock and Alan Condie, who frequently offered me a lift to school as they lived only a few houses away. Like many Southlanders, they were of Scottish descent, and had homes next door to each other. As I got to know them and their clan, they became my surrogate family and showered me with kindness during the two years I lived in Gore. Jock, especially, became the father I never had. He was an ex-Presbyterian minister, extremely erudite, with a wicked sense of fun and a penchant for pink gins. Once a week, we watched 'Z Cars' together through a haze of the aforementioned gin, and we talked and talked about everything under the sun. Jock had a passion for writing hilarious parodies based on Gilbert and Sullivan operas that mocked aspects of the education system. He really was brilliant. I adored him. His son, Alan, was also a very fine man and I had a secret crush on him for a long time. He had three beautiful children and a wonderful wife, Isobel. I loved them all dearly. People like these are a rare gift and a real treasure, a privilege to know, to be remembered, and valued all your life. They fed me, cared about me, watched over me, gave me love and friendship such as I had never known. For the first time in my life, I felt like I mattered to someone. I was truly blessed. But, at the end of the day, I still went home alone, to an empty house. I decided to get a dog.

Maggie, as I called her, became my best mate and companion during those two years in Gore, and we had some great times together. She was the sweetest pup, a collie labrador cross, and the shy one of her litter, which is why I chose her. I raised her from a small pup into a lovely, intelligent dog with a great nature. It wasn't easy having a dog when I worked all day, and my property wasn't fenced, so she got into a bit of strife with the local dog control authority. As usual, the Condies came to my rescue and Isobel babysat her during the day. I picked her up after school, bringing her home with me, but not before we'd enjoyed afternoon tea with Alan and Isobel. Maggie loved the Condies as much as I did, and the kids would often come down to take her for walks. When I finished in Gore, my father refused to let me bring her home, and I gave her to a farming family with a bunch of young kids. In retrospect, I should have kept Maggie and not returned home, branching out on my own at last. But I made the mistake of continuing to love people who gave me no love in exchange. How many times can your heart be broken? Now that I am old, I feel the battering my heart has taken over the years catching up on me, and some memories are just so hard to confront. I hope that Maggie had a happy life. The last time I saw her was when I visited Gore just before I went to Africa. I was shocked by how thin she was.

Shortly after I arrived in Africa, my parents got a dog.

Chapter Twelve

The two years I spent in Gore were not easy, but I still managed to notch up some memorable adventures. I used to organise bus trips for the kids to take them skating over winter, a massive logistical task which left me exhausted and for which the school expressed not a jot of thanks. Nowadays, you'd need a tome of risk management paperwork, letters from parents, and probably one from the Holy Ghost before you could set off on a similar jaunt, but back then nobody cared. Thank god I never lost a kid on my watch. They showed their gratitude by getting the captain of the school's first fifteen to bring me down in a bone crushing tackle while I was wobbling around out on the ice.

I also joined the school tramping club and went on day trips as well as full weekend ventures. Often, I was able to take Maggie along, and we saw lots of beautiful Southland and Otago countryside together. It was a good way to bond with kids and get to know staff. I had a solid pair of tramping boots, a backpack, and a little paraffin stove to cook on. I thought I was the female version of Barry Crump. Maggie shared my tent and was zipped into my sleeping bag with me.

My next-door neighbour in Christchurch, the one who'd helped me pay off my Uni debts by getting me the holiday job at the car dealership where he was a salesman, took pity on my having to make the tedious twelve-hour journey from Gore to Christchurch during school holidays by steam train and found me a little car, providing finance for it through his firm. Thus, I became the proud owner of a tiny beige Ford Prefect that I christened Clyde. On weekends, Myrlwynn, Maggie, Clyde, and I would head off up Central and explore great historical places like Arrowtown, Macetown, and Bendigo. We smuggled Mags into many a motel room. Clyde's engine, already tired when I bought him, blew up eventually, but it was relatively cheap to get a reconditioned one, and we were off again!

Southland was a land of plenty, and among other fond memories are trawling for flounders, gathering mussels, paua, and toheroas, picking autumn mushrooms fresh off the paddock, and harvesting wild blackberries to make blackberry and apple pie drowned with fresh cream. During duck shooting season, there were ducks to pluck and dress for the freezer, and when the Bluff oyster season opened, teachers like Alan would bring sacks of them into the staffroom and sell them to staff for thirty cents a dozen. A friend would often bring me muttonbirds, and we'd eat them with the grease dripping off our elbows. This was a land of infinite bounty, of milk and honey.

When school holidays came, I flogged Clyde doggedly up to Christchurch with Maggie asleep on the floor of the car's front passenger side, and I always took home a big sack of swedes, which sold on the roadside for fifty cents, for my parents. As soon as I arrived home, Mum followed an established pattern by taking to her bed with some mysterious, undiagnosed illness, and I took over the running of the house until she 'recovered'. I think she just seized the opportunity to have a break from running after my demanding father for a while. I didn't mind as I was used to the familiar ritual. I've always enjoyed cooking, and I took Maggie for long walks to get a break from the oppressive home atmosphere. I'm not sure why I went home for my school holidays at that time of my life. I guess it was just the same old misguided sense of loyalty.

Maggie had a little quirk, which meant she liked to dig holes in lawns. My father took a dim view of this as his garden was manicured to the nth degree, and eventually I had to leave Maggie in Gore for the holidays, with another dear friend, Kay Domigan. Kay, who was Scottish, had a lovely old springer spaniel, Pooch, who was much enamoured of Maggie, so it worked out well. Back in Gore, I had a regular Friday night dinner date with Kay. We shared food and wine and sorted the world out. She was much older than me, but the age difference didn't matter because we just clicked. She had married her New Zealand husband during the war, and the marriage was not a happy one. Les spent most of his time out carousing with the boys and Kay was lonely, like me, so we suited each other well. She was a very smart lady and I learned a lot from her. Her elder daughter had died tragically in a car crash, and I kind of became her surrogate daughter, I think. I was devastated when I received a letter in Africa from her surviving daughter telling me Kay had suffered a cerebral haemorrhage. She never fully recovered. I visited her after I returned home and gave her a gift of a little African carving, which seemed to delight her very much. She had a large hollow in her skull above her left eyebrow, the legacy of her illness and attendant surgery, and I came away feeling deeply distressed.

As far as the teaching went during my two years in Gore, it was odd, to say the least. This was before the digital age, when aged gestetner machines and carbon paper were used to make copies of things, so it was a time when you largely relied on 'chalk and talk'. New Zealand had an ineffectual Education Minister at the time – nothing new there – called Tallboys and whom we nicknamed 'Toyballs', and a desperate shortage of teachers. Totally unsuitable people without qualifications or relevant subject knowledge were rushed through pressure cooker training courses and issued with a 'TTC', Trained Teacher Certificate. Many of them did a fine job, but many did not. Professional standards were at an all time low, and teachers were disrespected and undervalued accordingly.

One good thing about Gore High was that there were no meetings (I still shudder at the memory of all the utterly demoralising, mind-numbingly pointless meetings I was forced to attend during my time as a teacher). The Rector 'didn't believe in them'. He was not running a democracy, apparently. Neither was my HOD, who was dedicatedly hands off, even by the Rector's standards. This meant you could pretty much teach anything you liked for as long as you liked. The only time you were expected to adhere to anything resembling a curriculum was the one dictated by the public exams: School Certificate and University Entrance. There were no appraisals, no accountability, no paperwork, apart from reports. The intolerable workloads and micro-management would come much later, as part of the spectacularly flawed 'Tomorrow's Schools'. Every educational philosophy seen to have failed overseas was avidly adopted by the New Zealand Ministry of Education, with predictable results.

For me, teaching was and always has been about the kids. Aware that I could not rely on the provocation of terror to maintain classroom discipline, I quickly learned to build good working relationships with the kids under my tutelage instead. This worked most of the time with most of the kids, but some kids would always be a penance, no matter who was teaching them. The class I remember most vividly in this respect was 4A, the bottom Fourth Form, thus designated so as not to give them the inferiority complex that being labelled 4Z(oo) would have, though it would certainly have been more apt. There were only about fourteen of them, but they were virtually unteachable, cooling their heels until they were legally old enough to leave and hire on at the Mataura freezing works (school leaving age then was fifteen), where they would earn way more money than me, as they frequently loved to remind me. Today, they'd be 'special needs', resourced accordingly, and with two or three teacher aides in the classroom to prevent the actual teacher going nuts. I had no such luxuries: no resources, no help, and no support.

The way I was allotted 4A was also an important life lesson that I internalised with much bitterness. My classroom was beside that of another first year teacher, Raelene Waddell. She taught languages, French, Latin and German, and so enjoyed classes with tiny student complements, especially at senior level. While I was dealing with classes of 25 to 30 kids, she enjoyed comparatively restful periods with classes numbering no more than 5 to 10 students maximum. She had the annoying habit of giving me pitying glances through the window in the door separating our two rooms, until I pasted some paper over it.

At the end of the first year, we were all given a list of our classes for the following one before school broke up for the summer holidays, and Raelene was given 4A, to keep her grounded in the real world, I assume. I was getting the usual mixed bag, while my HOD secured the best classes for himself, another common phenomenon in education, I was to learn. Raelene's response was to throw a massive tantrum, weeping and sobbing in the staffroom so that everyone had no doubt about the perilous emotional state that had been foisted on her by this aberration. The Rector liked her personally because they were in the same local choir and she was Presbyterian to boot. She was promptly relieved of the class and it was given to me. I accepted this state of affairs without protest because my family and teachers had done such a great job of destroying my self-esteem that I felt it was all I deserved. The whole staff knew it was unfair, and I made a mental vow to leave by the end of the next year, by which time I had hopefully saved enough money to go overseas.

I ended that first year of teaching with an appalling dose of the 'flu that left me skeletal and severely debilitated. Weeks passed before I felt even remotely like my old self again, and I struggled every day to climb the stairs to my classroom.

My dear friend, Myrlwynn, left for Australia, where she was due to be married, and I felt a deep sense of loss. We'd had some very good times together and kept each other sane during our first year of teaching. I'm not surprised that we are still good friends.

As anticipated, 4A were alarmingly feral. There were fourteen kids in the class, twelve boys and two girls, one of whom was a really nasty piece of work, but the boys mostly shut her down before I had to. Peer pressure is powerful. As their birthdays came around they left school, so the attrition rate was steady. They weren't bad kids, just victims of a system that made no provision for them and did not care about them. They could barely read or write, had the attention spans of gnats, and were not greatly interested in anything other than sex, booze, and thuggery. One boy frequently came to class hungover, the result of an alcoholic breakfast every morning, courtesy of his hard-drinking parents and their pals who obligingly left their dregs-filled classes lying around after yet another night of excess. I tried to come up with things that would interest them, but there were really no resources suitable for them, and I did not have the skills or know-how at this freshman stage of my education career to help them. My HOD took no interest when I appealed for help. I found out why he disliked me so much when I took over production of the school magazine. He told me I was not to put the 'Hons' after my MA 'as it wasn't the done thing in school mags' staff lists.' He was just the first one I encountered in a long line of petty individuals who suffered from professional jealousy

Floundering along without any guidance, I pitched 4A's lessons at more of a life-skills programme (I'd seen *To Sir With Love*), showing them, for example, how to write a letter for a job application, fill out forms, understand the basics of the Road Code, and copy down simple survival recipes. I tired to improve their literacy with some basic spelling and vocabulary. "If you don't have good language skills," I told them, "you can be manipulated by bad people." They looked at me with expressions of intense boredom.

One thing they did love, I discovered, was being read to. I found this book – I remember it was called *Bravik the Wolf Dog* – and started reading it to them one Friday afternoon, the time slot that saw them at their most restless, longing for the weekend. As I launched into the story, I sensed them gradually settling until the classroom became really quiet, all of them apparently focused on the unfolding plot. Delighted, I upped my game, putting more effort into expression, differentiating voices for the characters, and generally over-dramatising the whole narration. I could hear what sounded like muffled noises of wood splintering somewhere below us, but I was too carried away with my story-telling to really register them.

When I finally closed the book, just prior to the final bell for the week ringing, they were all sitting like statues, staring at me. My heart soared with new-found belief in my class management and teaching skills...until I realised to my horror that not one of them had a desk lid anymore. As the dreadful comprehension for these lacunae in my classroom furniture dawned, I ran to the windows, which were all opened since it was a warm autumn afternoon, peering out to see below the shards of kindling that used to be desk lids scattered on the concrete path that ran alongside the grass border fronting the street-side of the school. The explanation for the muffled sounds of wood shattering I'd registered while I was reading was now devastatingly clear. My classroom was on the second floor, so the classrooms below us, kids and teachers, would have had a good view as the lids cascaded down to splinter on the concrete. Then the final bell rang and my reprobates tore out the door before I could vent my outrage at this destructive behaviour. When I'd gathered my wits, I reported the incident and slunk home as fast as I could to indulge in a good cry, my sense of humiliation excruciating beyond words. I learned later that a few of the boys had brought screw drivers to class with them, probably purloined from the woodwork room, and while one removed the screws from his desk lid, willing hands conveyed them surreptitiously out the windows in a delinquent assembly line process. And I'd thought it was my brilliant choice of story, not to mention, my reading skills that had finally tamed the savage beast. Hubris indeed.

The Deputy Principal took 4A for a week, making them sit on the floor, even after the desk lids had been restored, as a punishment for the contempt they'd displayed towards school furniture, and by the time I returned to them they were in a very subdued mood, dare I say it, even remorseful. One of them gave me a nice roasting fowl, after putting the finishing touches to its plucking in his satchel on top of his desk. Another brought me some wood for my fire. I made sure I never took my eyes off the little buggers again, not for a nanosecond.

It took me a while to live down the incident of the desktops, but it sure made a good story to tell future classes, who always found it very entertaining. Raelene was, of course, predictably smug, but I doubt whether she would have fared any better with those feral kids. By the end of the year, my odd little group and I were all best mates, and I was ready to move on.

Chapter Thirteen

My second year at Gore High saw the arrival of a young teacher recruited from the UK, as many were in those days of teacher shortages, named Robin Parker. He was delightfully eccentric and infuriated the Rector by cooking bacon and eggs in his classroom as a three-dimensional prompt for a writing exercise about camping out.

On a Friday evening, a group of us celebrated the end of the week by getting together for a few drinks at Croydon Lodge, one of the local watering holes. Robin usually joined us, and I got to know him better. He'd worked in Africa, a country I had long yearned to visit, in Tanzania, teaching English at a little Catholic mission school run by German friars. I hung on his every word as he related tales of his experiences there, and he offered to give me a list of addresses, mostly taken from the Times Literary Supplement, that I could write to in my quest for a similar job. I had my heart set on going to Kenya. He was true to his word, and I carefully filed the addresses away for future reference. It was snail mail only back then.

I left Gore with little fanfare at the end of my second year there. I knew I would miss the Condies and Kay Domigan very much, but I vowed to keep in touch. I won't dwell on the parting from Maggie because it was so painful. I drove down to the Hollyford Valley for a few days and lost myself in the bush.

Once back in Christchurch, I found a job as a waitress and wondered where on earth my life was headed. Apart from Barry, I had not met a man that I felt in any way attracted to, while most of my friends were married and happily breeding, which state my mother made clear she expected me to emulate. But it held no attraction for me. I found those addresses Robin had given me and began to write. It was Africa or bust. In the meantime, I needed a job; any job.

Working as a waitress in a popular Christchurch motor lodge was an eye opener and certainly revealed an ugly side of human nature I'd not experienced before. It seemed the waitress, any waitress, was regarded as a particularly sub-human creature by many patrons, especially testosterone-fuelled groups of young men, who fed off their pack mentality rather than the food on their plates and appeared delighted when they reduced a young girl to a sobbing wreck. The chef, a short, aggressive Belgian named Werner, with glacial blue eyes and a pasty pockmarked complexion, was brutal in his chauvinism also, sexually harassing many of the girls, although he left me alone when he found out I was educated and a teacher. Complaints about him to the manager fell on deaf ears. We were told, 'He's my chef. I can always get waitresses.'

One day, while showing off his skill with a steel and carving knife, Werner's hand slipped and the razor sharp blade sliced open his forearm from wrist to elbow. This was my first experience of glorious karma. This guy who was always trying to impress us with how tough he was (he'd served in the Belgian armed forces, he claimed), screamed, howled, and thrashed about on the floor in a riveting display of infantile histrionics that splattered blood all over the kitchen. Mary, our hard-case breakfast cook who was built like a brick privy and pitiless as the result of a hard life, eventually sat on him to subdue him until the ambulance arrived. He was gone for days, much to our delight, and was sullenly mortified on his return; for a while, anyway, until he reverted to his old nasty self.

Six months of working in that wretched place left me with a lasting behavioural legacy, and I have made a point of treating waiting staff, shop assistants, check-out operators etc with kindness and respect ever since, cringing when others do not.

Answers to my pleas for a job in Africa began to trickle in and the theme was consistent: thanks but no thanks. I began to despair and to think about looking for another teaching job as I was fed up with being a waitress, a job for which I was eminently over-qualified and was doing my head in. One day I arrived home from work to find one of those thin little blue aerogrammes lying on the dining room table, addressed to me. My mum hovering nervously nearby, I opened it with trembling fingers and could hardly believe what I was reading. An organization based in Lusaka, Zambia, was offering me a contract to teach at a little Catholic mission school for African girls in a town called Livingstone (!). They were going to pay my airfare, provide me with a house, and I could come as soon as my work permit was issued. I was going to Africa! To a town named after Doctor Livingstone, a personal hero! I was deliriously happy – in stark contrast to my tight-lipped parent.

I don't think most people believed I was actually going to Africa, but I was. The contract documentation arrived along with a friendly personal letter from the principal of my intended school, Sister Carmel. I signed everything quickly and re-posted the paperwork, got my injections, got my passport, packed my belongings, booked my flight as soon as the work permit arrived and picked up my ticket. Handing in my notice at the motor lodge was especially sweet. To my surprise, they threw a little farewell party for me, gifting me with a lovely leather bound photo album and a silver and paua shell brooch shaped like my country.

I left New Zealand on a cold, wet day in July to begin the biggest adventure of my life. At the airport, my father took me aside and said, "If anything happens to you over there, I don't want to know about it. Don't expect me to help you out." As I stared at him in dismay, he added, "And don't put anything in your letters that will upset your mother." I looked after him in disbelief as he stalked off. I guess that was his idea of a fond farewell. He would never have dared to speak to any of my siblings like that, but he knew he could get away with it with me, since I had no value.

He wrote to me a couple of times when I was in Africa, always signing himself 'Dad', never 'Love, Dad'. Mind you, if he had signed 'Love, Dad', I would have been sickened by the hypocrisy. Self-love, narcissism, was the closest he ever came to that particular emotion.

My time in Africa is fully documented in my book, *Expat Blues*, still a work in progress, which is heartily recommended to the future reader. The first three months were hard as I struggled with culture shock and excruciating homesickness. My father's parting words had made it clear that I could expect no reprieve, so I had to duke it out and eventually I settled in, made friends, and began, with the support of my exceptional principal, to enjoy the experience.

Suffice it to say, I had a memorable, action-packed thirty months there and too many amazing experiences to recount in this space. Some of the highlights included a marriage proposal from a smitten Italian, finally losing my virginity, a near-death brush with cerebral malaria (just like Henry Morton Stanley), an 8,000km safari up to East Africa and back in a tinny little Japanese car with three equally reckless Irish girls, being arrested at the South African border, and narrowly escaping, by way of a hair-raising car ride, from the law at the Zambia/Rhodesia border, with a fistful of illegal money. That particular exploit passed into local legend and required the help of the town's police chief – an expat Irishman, luckily for me – to sort out. I always pushed my courage beyond an acceptable level, one way of clawing back the self-esteem that had been stripped from me. (The local expats called me 'the crazy Kiwi', with a not-undeserved reputation for having problems at borders). It was the greatest time of my life, and the most rewarding teaching experience. I was appointed Head of English at the beautiful little St Mary's School, and some of my students gained the best exam results in the whole country.

I came home again at the end of 1974 feeling very conflicted about doing so, as my heart remained in Africa, but I still retained that misguided loyalty to my family, loving those who did not care about me. I had sent them many beautiful gifts from Africa during my contract period; carvings, clothing, artefacts, exotic presents I could barely afford on my meagre salary. But I know now that, with certain people, generosity and kindness does not necessarily earn you love or alter in any way your value to them.

Of course, after nearly three year's away, I was bound to notice changes. In my absence, and after repudiating the demon drink all her life because of what she had witnessed of its effects on her parents, my mother's genetic disposition had finally caught up with her and she had become a full-blown alcoholic who began drinking at ten o'clock every morning and continued to do so steadily all day, until she crawled off to bed thoroughly sozzled while it was still daylight. It was terrible to watch her staggering past in her voluminous flannel nightgown with her Maltese terrier tucked under one arm, insensible to its biting and snarling at being thus forcibly abducted to bed so early. My father seemed oblivious to her almost permanent state of drunkenness. He was his usual obnoxious self, refused to look at any of my photos or slides from Africa, and tried to humiliate me every night at the dinner table. His ritual went something like this: first, he'd look me up and down before sneeringly pronouncing, "MA Honours! Huh!" Then he'd dredge up some obscure topic he knew a little about and proceed to lecture me on it. All his mind-numbing perorations began with the same formula: 'They tell me...' 'They' had a lot to answer for. Meanwhile, Mum crouched in an inebriated heap at the end of the table, doing the frowning thing she did with her oddly sparse, drink-inflamed eyebrows, which meant, "Don't contradict him. Keep the peace." It was a dismal period, but eventually my sister and I managed to get Dad to put all the booze under lock and key and Mum gradually sobered up. The saddest thing for me was witnessing that, when intoxicated, she was every bit as nasty and aggressive as Dad. *In vino veritas.*

Two of my father's deeds from this time stand out. When it became clear that my mother's beloved but elderly Maltese was going to start costing vet's fees to maintain, Dad poisoned him with snail bait. When he became distressingly ill, he whipped him off the vet for euthanasia. The other incident is seared into my memory, and is like a metaphor for my father himself, for his intrinsic nature: the cherry tree.

All the time we were growing up, we had a beautiful cherry tree flourishing in our backyard. Every spring it was an explosion of cascading, snowy blossom that filled the whole garden with its spicy musk. I liked to sit under it and read a book.

One afternoon, without warning, a mate of my father's turned up with a chainsaw, and I watched in horror-stricken disbelief as the perfectly healthy tree was brutally dismembered, its butchered segments scattered across the lawn. Only a bleeding stump remained. Mum fled to the bedroom. When everything had been cleared up and the mate with the saw had left, Dad strolled into the kitchen, poured himself a whiskey, sipped, smacked his lips, raised his glass as if he were drinking to a dead acquaintance, and said, "Ahhhh! I enjoyed that." I had never before felt so repulsed by him as I did at that moment.

My misguided quest for love and affection saw me make the saddest mistake of all during this troubled hiatus in my life. I had a brief affair with a married man and fell pregnant. I knew there would be no family support forthcoming, so I had an abortion, something I will always regret deeply, although I would never pass judgement on any woman who has to make this painful decision. While I believe a woman should have autonomy over her own body, my awareness of the moral issues at stake, especially with my Catholic upbringing, has left me deeply conflicted over this sad experience

My brother Mike was away teaching in Invercargill, and Sean was in the army training as a chef. I longed to get away, too. I was supposed to go on to a job in Columbia after a period of rest and recuperation, but that did not eventuate. I instead signed a contract with an Australian company, to go and teach on the island of Nauru, but I never made it, getting married instead, settling down to domesticity and raising a family...what Nikos Kazantzakis (*Zorba the Greek*) called 'the full catastrophe'. I met my husband, Phil, who predictably became the butt of much nastiness and viciousness from my family, when I went back into teaching and accepted a job at a school in Auckland. He did have an abrasive personality at times, but no allowance was ever made by my kin, especially my sister, for the tragic childhood he had endured, and which I hope to write a book about eventually. (Five minutes after meeting him, my sister said to me, "He's got a nose like a ski run.")

He was flavour of the month, though, much later, when he risked his job at Auckland airport to send food parcels we could ill afford to her and her husband on outgoing flights to Samoa, after they dragged their four boys off there for two miserable, hard-up years they bitterly regretted. Most contracted couples leave third world countries when they start a family; they actually uprooted theirs and took them *to* a third world country.

Phil was, to begin with, my flatmate, and while it wasn't love at first sight, we gradually became enamoured of each other and I accepted his proposal. He was a big, kind, exuberant guy, half Italian, larger than life and side-splittingly funny. We weren't really compatible, but we stayed together for twenty-one years until his untimely death from cancer.

At the conclusion to my wedding day, as my new husband and I prepared to leave for our wedding night venue, my mother curled her lip and snarled at me, "You're in a hurry, aren't you?" That single, derisive slur with its nasty implication that I was an oversexed slut ruined my entire day in an instant.

The following morning, Phil wanted to call in home, for reasons that escaped me, before we set off on our honeymoon. I think he truly believed that my family would take him into their bosom, whereas I knew only too well that, being my husband, he would be as valueless as I was. As we walked into the house, I was arrested by the sight of my father hastening towards me, arms outstretched, with what could only be described as an expression of stupefied lust on his face. This man, who had never embraced me in his life, clasped me to him and planted a wet, sloppy kiss on my lips, as if he could experience by proxy any sexual activity I'd enjoyed with my husband on our wedding night. I recoiled in disgust, wiping my lips. Over his shoulder I caught my mother's eye and she quickly looked away. It still makes me shudder to think about it.

For our first Christmas as man and wife, my husband and I returned home to Christchurch. On Christmas Day, my mother found a bottle of Bourbon that my brother, Michael, had bought. Chug-a-lugging from the bottle, she quickly morphed into her nasty, aggressive persona and began to verbally abuse Phil, telling me in a slurred voice that he was 'Nothing but a Pom' (NZ slang for an English person.) In fact, he was the son of an English father and an Italian mother, and had been born in Egypt. Drunk or sober, she would never have dreamed of talking about my sister's husband that way, despite his German blood. The following day, sobered up, she refused to apologise and went about with an air of self-righteous indignation.

On yet another dismal Christmas Day, I watched my father approach Phil holding out a bottle of Chianti, which, true to his Italian heritage, my husband loved. As Phil reached to take it, smiling with delight, my father suddenly veered away, handing it instead to one of his grandsons and calling over his shoulder with an ugly sneer, "I bet you thought it was for you, didn't you?" Yes, indeed, always knew how to make Christmas memorable.

When I fell pregnant with my second child, I rang my parents to tell them my good news. My father answered the phone, and I told him the reason for my call. He snorted and said, "You randy bitch."

I had two children, a son, Ben, and a daughter, Francesca, and eventually returned to work, teaching fifty years all up, the last eighteen, with some interruptions, in special needs, mainly supporting deaf students. It was hard on many levels, but left me with some positive memories.

Both my children were born in Auckland, and when they were little we moved back to Christchurch, another dreadful mistake I made, and once again triggered by my loyalty to the family who cared nothing for me. The move brought only further heartache and bitterness. We had three happy years on a small farm out at Broomfield in North Canterbury, and I wanted to stay there forever amongst our pet sheep, goat and horses, but it was not to be. My husband was not a country boy, and things got complicated when the kids reached high school age and there was a dearth of desirable institutions locally. So, we moved back into town. Not long afterwards, Phil became terminally ill. His sad childhood should have guaranteed him a long, happy old age by way of compensation, but life is rarely fair like that. Witnessing his dreadful suffering and subsequent death was devastating and shook my Christian faith to its foundations. It has taken twenty-two years to revive.

At Phil's funeral, my mother, also widowed at this point, offered me not a single word of comfort. It was not all about her, so she was indifferent.

After my father retired, he and my mother had a difficult period of adjustment without any children there to provide a buffer, and Mum's whining about him became incessant. He didn't help his cause by using some money he'd inherited from his late sister Nell's estate, to take himself for a holiday to the United States, leaving Mum behind. Her bitterness reached critical mass. His conscience must have pricked him because he made another trip later on, and this time Mum accompanied him. One story she subsequently told about the experience presumably summed up their tour. When they stopped over in Las Vegas, Dad insisted they retire to bed at

6.30 p.m., to prevent her playing the pokies, of course. Mum said she sat on the edge of her bed, staring out the hotel window until it grew dark...in Las Vegas.

Dad went downhill in his eighties, drinking heavily and becoming increasingly irrational. He developed dementia, becoming even more challenging to deal with, and finally causing my mother to have a mild breakdown. We had no choice but to place him in a dementia care unit, where Mum barely visited him, and where he passed away after two years spent cut off from the family he'd taken so for granted. I visited him the day before he died and he was exhibiting that bizarre phenomenon of dying people where they have a last, desperate burst of energy, its expression for him taking the form of his repeatedly trying to get up out of his chair and continually falling back, his face contorted with rage and frustration. He suddenly seemed to notice me and his expression changed to a hideous leer. "Pull your pants down," he snarled at me. Those were my father's last words to me, words that vindicated the prurience I had always intuited, and that had always repulsed me and made me uneasy around him. When I told my sister, she hooted with laughter.

Shortly after our father's death, the younger of my two brothers, Sean, fell victim to the mental illness that often strikes down members of large families of Irish heritage, and certainly afflicts ours. Although his male gender had protected him to a large degree from the negativity that blighted my upbringing, I think he had his own issues after just being born too late to by then indifferent parents. For a while, after leaving school, he had worked in my father's asphalting business, where he was mercilessly bullied by the foreman, behaviour my father witnessed, but did nothing to address. Joining the army to train as a chef eventually freed Sean from this negative work environment, although clearly damage had been done. He did a stint in Singapore and seemed to have found a niche in the military. It was after he left the army that he struggled. He had a schizophrenic breakdown in his late twenties, which culminated in his divorce from his Chinese wife, whom he'd married in Singapore, and estrangement from his only child, a son, and came back to Christchurch where he moved in with Mum, then living on her own after Dad's death.

Now in his sixties, Sean has been unemployed since his late twenties, and although clearly intellectually impaired also, he is good about taking his meds and copes as well as can be expected. Mum's pregnancy with him and his subsequent birth were difficult, probably leaving him with neural damage. He arrived into a family already set in its ways, with the major roles already allotted: crown princess, scapegoat, golden child. Born late to aging parents, there was only one role left for him to fill: the lost child. Mellowed out on his meds, he has always put me in mind of a larger version of the little dwarf, Dopey, who trails after his fellows in the movie *Snow White*, smiling benignly and carrying the lantern...tail end Charlie. I think he may be a lot like our grandfather, John Anderson, who had a similar aversion to work.

Once Sean was diagnosed and prescribed the correct medication, he settled into a placid, if somewhat aimless existence, of dependence on the State. So, for the last six years of her life our mother had a quiet, biddable man to keep her company, look after her and cook for her, before she herself developed dementia and went into care, where she passed away six months later.

My brother, Michael, married a divorcee with two daughters later in life and had no children of his own. We were close as children, but in later years he has gravitated firmly towards my sister. I find this ironic, as she never had any time for him growing up and put him down almost as often as she did me. The difference was that he was better than me at standing up to her, and, crucially, Mum came to his defence. But the two favourites are anyway bound to share an affinity by virtue of their privileged status.

One incident that brought home to me with brutal clarity how deeply inculcated was my inferior status within my family occurred a couple of years after I returned home from Brunei. My brother Michael's elder stepdaughter was getting married, and his three siblings plus my sister's husband duly travelled to Queenstown, where he and his wife lived, to attend this happy event. After a lovely church service we wandered across to the restaurant where the reception was being held. At the entrance to the dining room was a seating plan showing where the guests would be seated at individual tables, and I was brought back to Earth with a thump. While my sister and her husband were seated at a table with my brother and his wife, along with other VIP guests, Sean, whom both our siblings knew full well has no conversation whatsoever, and I were relegated to a separate table with a group of the bride's relatives, all total strangers who, after the initial formalities, ignored us. Thus, I realised that my role for the evening was to babysit Sean and that any compromise to my enjoyment that might ensue from that situation was of no consequence. Why would it be? As a person I did not matter. I never had. It struck me forcefully then, that the non-person status I had endured growing up in my family was no way altered or abolished by my parent's deaths: it was my well-established heritage and it was going to continue for my whole life.

In summary, although my brothers never actively scapegoated me the way my parents and sister did, neither did they ever defend me, and still don't. By the time they arrived and were old enough to be aware, my role in the family had already been well and truly determined, so for them, I guess, it was just situation normal, the status quo.

Our family legacy is that there are no strong bonds of love that hold us together because they were never nurtured in the first place, during our formative years. Our whole *modus vivendi* was one of keeping up superficial appearances, of dissimulation as we played out our ascribed roles, and presiding over it all was our mother with her relentless mantra: 'Keep the peace.' All our small, familial world was, indeed, a stage.

****

My son, his wife, and my two lovely grandchildren live nearby and I would be lost without them. Tragically, my daughter has also succumbed to the mental health issues that plague our family, and has cut herself off from us, making me the scapegoat – I seem unable to shake that role – for all her self-loathing and her sad pattern of shattered relationships, an additional heartbreak I could have done without. The last time I tried to reconcile with her, she assaulted me yet again, and my sister quickly seized an opportunity to hurt me by taking her side, delivering the final blow to what had always been a tenuous relationship. I wasn't really surprised, because my sister has assaulted me, too. We had a falling out on my father's eightieth birthday, just after I'd returned to Christchurch with my family, and she slapped my face and pulled my hair, a regression to our childhood, I guess, where she dominated me, with Mum's approval. (When I'd arrived at the party, wearing one of my colourful, traditionally patterned tops I'd bought in Africa, she addressed me thus: "You look like you've come from a bazaar." And what did I say, in response to this insult? Nothing, as per usual.) But later on that night, I did stand up to her, and she was shocked to her core. Also unsurprising was that my mother took her side. But it was a crucial turning point for me: at last, I had begun to fight back. When we eventually reconciled after that little fracas, my sister had sadly learned nothing. She told me I was never to wear my particular African ensemble again, including the shell earrings. They had offended her, apparently. Why? Did they symbolise my deeper, richer life experience, a threat to her entrenched view of me as a pathetic loser, someone to be despised and pitied? That was the role she had always assigned me, after all.

My mother later told me that she did not think such confrontations as occurred between my sister and me 'would ever happen in my family'. This was my opportunity to enlighten her on how she had laid the groundwork for such a showdown over many years, but her rigid self-righteousness would never have allowed her to countenance such a cold home truth.

In retrospect, it is better not to confront the ones who have habitually hurt you, because they will never own their behaviour, blaming their victim instead. That is how bullies and scapegoaters work. It is better to remove yourself from them altogether, and this is what the experts also recommend. Anyway, I now refer to my sister and my daughter as 'The Fight Club'. (My daughter inevitably turned on her, as well. All too predictable.)

After my husband passed away with cancer in 1997, leaving me a widow at fifty, I went to Brunei for two years, again earning the wrath of my sister who accused me of being a bad mother and abandoning my kids. I had, in fact, the blessings of both, now grown up and living with partners, and was simply trying to pay off the five-figure mortgage my husband's death had left me to deal with on my own. Apart from my own two kids, not a single member of my close family came to see me off.

Brunei was no cakewalk, but I earned good money there because teachers were paid well without being overworked, and there was no tax. I also did a lot more travelling, going as far as England, Israel, and all over Asia, and I flew both my children over for holidays with me. When I came home briefly at the end of my first year away, my sister snubbed me when we met up at a nephew's engagement party. My mother died at the end of my second year there, (my father having passed away several years earlier) and I missed her funeral. I thought that was probably pretty fitting. She was never there for me.

I do not go to either of their graves.

In 2010, 2011, Christchurch was hit by a series of devastating earthquakes from which the city is still recovering. I lost my home, but 182 people lost their lives. The 'quakes changed us all, but life goes on. Anyway, that's another whole story. (I'm never going to get them all done before I shuffle off this mortal coil!)

I retired at the age of 67, but kept on working with one dyslexic student until I was 72. Now, I am a dedicated author, who has published seven books and one short story in an American collection. I have never remarried and wear my aloneness as my shield and armour. It is, I believe, my natural condition. Unashamedly now, I wear my heart on my sleeve. Writing is my therapy.

There has always been an empty space beside me. The dear friend, the lover, the soulmate has never arrived to fill it. I know what he looks like. I *will* find him. Maybe in my next life…..

Epilogue

"Tragedy is written distinct and small." James K Baxter

As I pointed out at the beginning of this story, life is a bit of a lottery, and the family you end up in is certainly a game of chance, a game you have no control over. You are a conscious being inside a body that could be born to anyone. You come into this world alone, you live your life essentially alone, irrespective of whoever else may he orbiting around you, and you make the final journey alone. This sounds rather bleak, but I do not intend it to be. Life is still an amazing gift and I count my blessings every day, acknowledging that there are souls in this world who have suffered far worse trauma. To each person, of course, he/she is the world.

Many people fall victim to differential parenting and, if they read my story, they will be able to recognise and affirm my pain as mirroring their own. I suffered physical, emotional, and psychological abuse, the effects of which were exacerbated by my ultra-sensitive, intuitive, imaginative nature, but I have, I believe, risen above the lasting pain, have lived a good life, and have achieved much despite a hard battle against a childhood legacy that left me with low esteem and no sense of self worth. I firmly believed I was of no value to anyone, and my life experience confirmed this at every turn. I began to wonder if I had the word 'victim' tattooed on my forehead. Well, I did, and my family put it there. When people intuit this vulnerability, their worst predatory instincts are aroused and they zero in on what they believe is a soft target, which I was. I met many such people in the teaching profession, and it took me a while before I drew a line in the sand and fought back to preserve my personal dignity. When I did, I won hands down, surprising quite a few. I am, after all, of Irish descent, and the Irish know how to fight! (and write!) Somebody wisely said, 'never piss off a writer'! They might preserve your bad behaviour for posterity. There are a couple of my skirmishes that will make great short stories. Stick around.

What will always hurt, is knowing that the very people who should have loved me, cared about me and protected me, were the very ones who betrayed me, hurt me, and damaged me. Well, to all of you I say, I am all right, and it's your loss, not mine. What happened to me in my family, set me up for a life made harder by the lack of confidence and self-pride my childhood instilled in me. With the help of counselling and personal faith, I believe I have finally overcome those barriers, and I hope my story helps others who have experienced the pain of being scapegoated and unfavoured make a similar comeback. Human nature can be an ugly thing, but you can beat it if you keep hold of your courage, if you don't let the tormentors win, and if you remove yourself to a place they can no longer reach you. Sadly, for some this place is suicide, which brings home with a punch just how devastating the consequences can be. I will always wonder what kind of a person I would be, whether my life would have turned out differently, if I had grown up with people who validated me, instead of dismantling me. I've come a long way, but I'm still working to reassemble myself, and will be until the day I die. The fracture lines will always be evident to the more sensitive and caring, who have been somewhat of a dearth in my life.

Finally, I have a theory I will share with you. In the days of the cavemen, the hunter-gatherers, life was harsh, and the sensitive, artistic members of the tribe, the star-gazers and dreamers were regarded with contempt by those who valued brawn over brain as being the essential for survival in a harsh world. So the dreamers took themselves off to the rear of the cave where they drew their pictures, made up their songs and stories, and stored the music of the world in their hearts. They knew they would always be the outsiders, regarded with amusement or contempt by the jocks and pragmatists. This did not concern or upset them, because they knew they would leave a more meaningful heritage for their descendants, something more precious than bones and middens and weapons, something that makes human beings absolutely unique – imagination.

.

ABOUT THE AUTHOR

I live in Christchurch, New Zealand. The city is still rebuilding after the devastating earthquakes of 2010 and 2011, which destroyed my home. I have been a teacher for most of my life, most recently a teacher of deaf students and those with special needs. I've taught overseas as well, in Africa and in Brunei. I have two children, one of whom, my daughter, lives in the North Island while the other, my son, lives here in Christchurch with my two grandchildren. I started writing five years ago and have completed eight books: a contemporary romance, three war stories, two books in a medieval fantasy trilogy, and this, my most recent one. I have many more ideas for stories yet to come.

Made in the USA
Las Vegas, NV
14 January 2021